SPORTS ARCHITECTURE

DESIGN MEDIA PUBLISHING LIMITED

The significance of Legacy in the design of tomorrow's major sports facilities

—Richard Breslin

Major sports facilities often built for an international event. An event creates a huge global opportunity to showcase a city through a major stadium to millions of people around the world but equally important is the building's legacy afterwards. What's left behind after the main event should be as sustainable as it is beautiful, and that is sustainable in a widest possible sense - economically, socially and environmentally? Sometimes the sports facility might not even be permanent, and it can be disassembled after the event, taken away and built somewhere else, for another major event.

Populous is honoured to write this preface for the book Sports Architecture for Liaoning Science and Technology Publishing House. As members of the construction industry in the developed world, we feel particularly responsible for the environment, and as specialists and leaders in the design of major sports and entertainment buildings, we continually look for ways to approach the construction of the buildings sustainably. The key principal is that sports stadia are huge pieces of infrastructure and when it comes to sustainable design; their use of energy is a major issue. The industry must learn to reduce the energy use in their initial construction – the so-called "embodied energy" and to later reuse the building materials in future projects.

The Sydney stadium for the 2000 Olympic Games set the benchmark for the modern sustainable stadium. It was the largest Olympic stadium ever built and as Sydney was the Green Games, the stadium included innovative sustainable design measures such as passive ventilation and collection of rainwater, now included in stadium design everywhere.

London began to examine these issues immediately after it won the right to stage the Olympic Games for 2012. London already had Wembley stadium, it didn't need a second national stadium. London has also learnt from Sydney that it can take 10 years to turn a dedicated Olympics stadium into a truly useful community resource so legacy was considered right at the beginning and the Government established a legacy company to plan for all Olympic venues after the Games.

At the same time legacy was considered, so too were construction methods and materials. What emerged at the end of the design process was a watershed in stadium design: a building that is flexible, lightweight, and semi-temporary, yet one that still makes a statement as the landmark stadium for the grand ceremonies of the London 2012 Olympics. It is designed to be reconfigured after the Games into a smaller stadium for soccer. It is the most environmentally friendly Olympic stadium ever built, using less steel than any other comparable Olympic stadium. It also has a roof made of fabric. The construction methods and materials meant the stadium was also built ahead of schedule. Construction began in 2008 and it was completed in March 2011. The London Olympic Stadium will also be one of

the fastest buildings to transform itself from Olympic mode to a profitable, sustainable post Olympic venue.

The lessons learned from London are now being translated into the design of the Olympic stadium for the Sochi 2014 Winter Games, which is the third Olympic stadium being designed by Populous. Legacy design is as important in a community stadium as it is in an Olympic stadium. Dunedin, in New Zealand, for example faced a particular dilemma building its new stadium. It is one of the most southerly cities in the world, and its cold, wet climate posed particular challenges. A big city might have a budget to afford moving tiers and opening and closing roof which would be an ideal solution in such circumstances. But Dunedin needed a smaller community stadium, with 20,000 permanent seats, and there was never going to be enough money in the budget to build a fully enclosed roof, or to cover the expense of bringing grass pallets in and out of the stadium for games.

So after many years of research, an innovative solution was found - enclosing a natural turf stadium in a specially engineered plastic. Forsyth Barr was officially opened in August 2011 and is the world's only permanently enclosed natural turf stadium featuring a space age, transparent roof clad in ETFE, a transparent polymer or plastic. The ETFE covering is light, enclosed and translucent, allowing maximum sunlight onto the pitch, so that the grass keeps growing but the fans are protected from the elements whatever the weather. Once again the lessons learnt from earlier work, this time, enclosing the centre court at Wimbledon, in London, provided important insights to what would be needed in Dunedin.

We believe that a stadium, more than any other building type in history, has the ability to shape a town or city. A stadium is able to put a community on the map, establishing an identity and providing a focal point in the landscape. Stadias are the most "viewed" buildings in history and have the power to change people's lives: they represent a nation's pride and aspirations. They can be massively expensive to build, but they can also generate huge amounts of money. Consequently the stadium will become the most important building any community can own, and if it is used wisely, it will be the most useful urban planning tool a city can possess. Designing for adaptability and legacy, with innovation and a respect for the environment – these are the key ingredients in major sports facilities of the future.

Contents

Large-scale

6   *Shenzhen Bay Sports Centre*

12   *Bao'an Stadium 56*

18   *Moses Mabhida Stadium*

26   *Cape Town Stadium*

30   *Astana Arena*

34   *Metricon Stadium*

40   *Wembley Stadium*

46   *Forsyth Barr Stadium, Dunedin*

52   *Universiade 2011 Sports Centre*

58   *Shanghai Oriental Sports Centre*

64   *Gobela Sports Complex*

70   *Bilbao Arena and Sports Centre*

76   *Arena Zagreb*

80   *Coliseums for South American Games*

Professional

84   *The Joan Gamper Training Facility for FC Barcelona*

88   *Soccer Stadium Nueva Balastera*

92   *Carnegie Pavilion*

98   *Sports Hall - FK Austria Wien Training Academy*

102 *Slowtecture M*

108 *Queensland Tennis Centre*

112 *New Sports Hall*

118 *EMÜ Sports Hall*

126 *Zamet Centre*

136 *Podčetrtek Sports Hall*

144 *Orense Swimming Pools for Vigo University*

148 *Municipal Polls of Povoação*

156 *Expansion of Centre Sportif J.C. Malépart*

164 *Torre Pellice Ice Palace*

170 *Majori Primary School Sports Ground*

Complex

176 *Multifonctional Complex 'La Maladiere'*

184 *Aberdeen Sports Village*

192 *Futian Sports & Entertainment Complex*

196 *Berry Sports and Recreation Hall*

202 *University of Maine Student and Recreation Centre*

208 *University of Wisconsin Oshkosh Student Recreation and Wellness Centre*

214 *California State University, Long Beach, Student Recreation & Wellness Centre*

220 *East Campus Athletic Village*

226 *Sports City Hall Bale*

230 *University of Arizona Student Recreation Expansion*

236 *Drexel University Recreation Centre*

242 *Tianjin Sports Arena*

248 *Sollentuna Swimming and Sports Centre Extension*

254 *Chimo Aquatic and Fitness Centre*

262 *Birkerod Sports and Leisure Centre*

268 *Curtin Stadium*

274 *Deodoro Sports Complex*

280 *Ronald McDonald Centre*

287 *Index*

Shenzhen Bay Sports Centre

Designer: BIAD+AXS SATOW inc. **Architects:** Bing Wang, Xiaoli Kang, Yizhi Fu **Location:** Shenzhen, China **Completion:** 2011 **Photographer:** Chaoying Yang, Shaoming Xie **Building area:** 335,298m²

Shenzhen Bay Sports Centre is located in the middle of Shenzhen Bay waterfront recreational district, northeast of the Nanshan Sea central district, in the Reclamation area of Shenzhen Bay and the southern edge of Binhai Avenue. It is adjacent to Keyuan Road to the west, Shahe West Road to the east, and inner lake of Shenzhen Bay to the south. Its west-east length is 720 metres, and north-south width is 430 metres. The total site area is 30.77 hectares, and total floor area is 326,000 square metres. Shenzhen Bay Sports Centre is the main venue of the 26th Summer Universiade held in Shenzhen 2011, taking the opening ceremony, table tennis finals, swimming competition and training functions. As major sports building complex, the centre facilities mainly include a stadium with 20,000 seats for audiences, a sports hall with 13,000 seats, a swimming hall with 650 seats, athletes reception centre, sports theme park and business operation facilities. After the universiade, the centre will be a sports and fitness venue for citizens of Nanshan district besides holding some of national comprehensive competitions, special competitions and sports training activities. Here will become a large comprehensive sports complex integrating competitive matches, fitness, leisure travel and trade expo activities.

As a new building complex located in Qianhai-Houhai district, which is one of the "Double Centres" of Shenzhen, Shenzhen Bay Sports Centre not only fully coordinates with the surrounding urban planning, and will also become an urban landmark of Nanshan district due to its spectacular, beautiful and extended pattern.

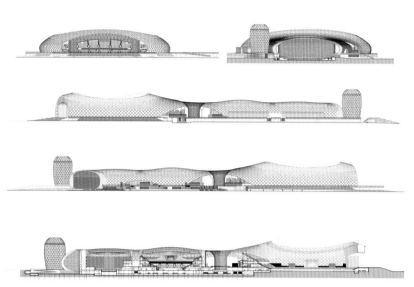

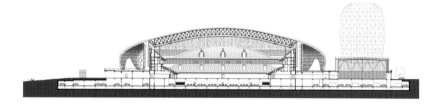

1. The sport centre -"Cocoon" in the dark
2. Bird view of the sport centre
3. View of the sports hall from west Sunken Plaza

1

2

1. The Stadium
2. Gate of Sea
3. Audience platform

1. Stadium
2. Water pond
3. Rooms for competitions
4. Warm-up courts
5. Outdoor parking
6. Athletes reception centre
7. Tennis hall
8. Warm-up hall
9. Commercial rooms
10. The Tree Square
11. Gymnasium
12. Natatorium
13. Sunken plaza
14. Audiences entrance plaza

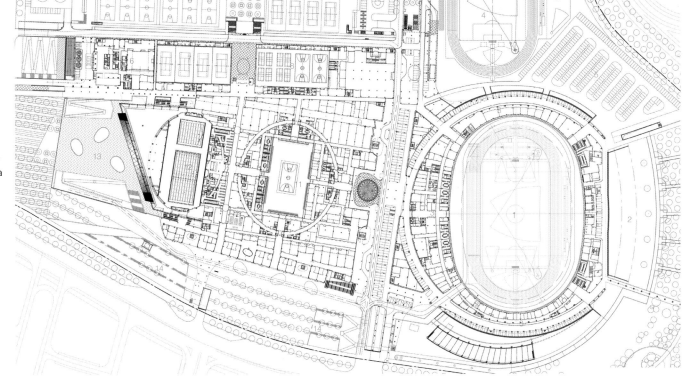

1. The Tree Plaza
2. Stadium interior
3. Heart of the Tree Plaza

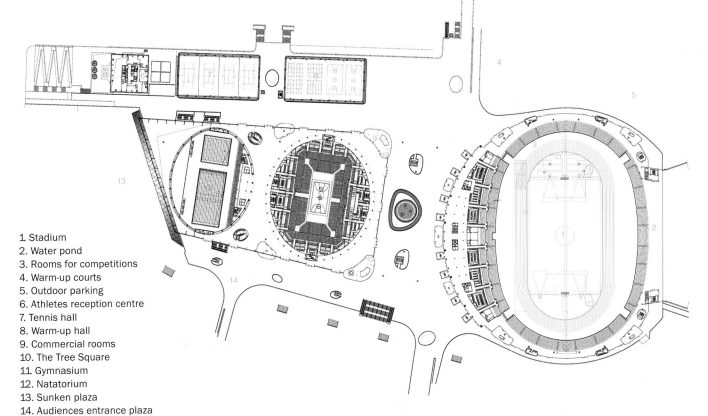

1. Stadium
2. Water pond
3. Rooms for competitions
4. Warm-up courts
5. Outdoor parking
6. Athletes reception centre
7. Tennis hall
8. Warm-up hall
9. Commercial rooms
10. The Tree Square
11. Gymnasium
12. Natatorium
13. Sunken plaza
14. Audiences entrance plaza

Bao'an Stadium

Designer: gmp - von Gerkan, Marg and Partners Architects **Chinese partner practice:** SCUT South China University of Technology **Location:** Shenzhen, China **Completion:** 2011 **Photographer:** Christian Gahl **Building area:** 88,500 m²

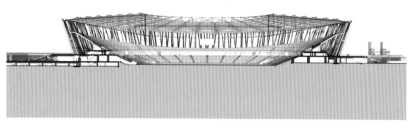

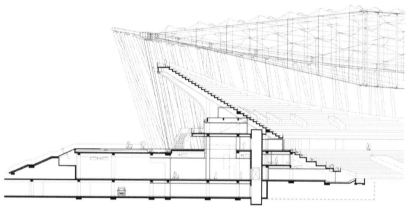

For several weeks, the summer Universiade in Shenzhen, north of Hong Kong in the Pearl River Delta on the Chinese mainland, focused world attention on the up-and-coming city. The stadium (actually in the Bao'an district) is designed as an athletics stadium holding 40,000 spectators. However, during the 2011 Universiade, it was being used for football matches.

The extensive bamboo forests of southern China were the inspiration for the design. The bamboo look serves two purposes. It reflects the character of the region, and thus creates identity. And it serves as a structural concept for both the load-bearing frame of the stadium stands and the supports for the wide-span roof structure. The outermost part of the stadium unites façade, structure and overarching architectural theme in a single feature. The natural look of the bamboo forest, together with the interplay of light and shadow between the trunks, is interpreted structurally through rows of slender steel supports, as outsize, abstract versions of the bamboo shape.

The stadium is located in the immediate vicinity of a sports arena and swimming bath, which have already established an east-west axis. The stadium and the attached warming-up place fall in with this existing urban axis. The choice of a pure circle for the geometry of the stadium was a decision not to introduce any other geographical orientation into the urban-planning situation, and to emphasize the central character of the sports venue. Appropriately for the uses of the building, the stadium stands on a grassed plinth, which incorporates on the inside the lower tiers of seating and internal functional areas.

The geometry of the spectator seats involves a modulation from the oval of the athletics track into a perfect circle. The undulating upper tier of the stands is the result of this modulation, creating a large number of seats on the long sides of the pitch and fewer seats on the short sides. The curved line of the upper edge of the stands is repeated by the overall shape of the stadium.

Visitors to a sports event access the stadium via broad flights of steps that lead up to the podium on four sides. The flat podium allows free circulation around the whole stadium and easy access to the seats from any side. Visitors pass through the forest of steel supports into the first circulating area of the stadium, and thence go either up the steps to the upper tier or straight on to the top of the lower tier. The image of a bamboo forest is created by the double row of steel supports, which come across as irregularly spaced and angled as in a real forest. Every other support in the inner row is connected with the concrete structure of the undulating upper tier, thus carrying the vertical loads of the spectator seating.

Though the supports for the roof structure stand inside the rows of stand supports, they are completely separate from the concrete structure in order to cater for independent movements in the large roof. The steel tubes, which are up to 32 metres in length, differ qualitatively according to their load-bearing behaviour and function. In diameter, they range from 550 millimetre to 800 millimetre, varying in accordance with their differing static loads. The horizontal stiffening of the structure and drainage of the roof membrane is likewise provided by special supports.

Particular attention was also paid to the efficient use of materials during the design of the roof structure of the Bao'an Stadium, as a fundamental principle of sustainable building. This is why a membrane roof suspended from an outer frame was selected to cover the seating areas – the ratio of material used to the surface covered constitutes an ingenious optimum for wide-span structures.

1. Bird view of the building in the daytime
2. Exterior view from the side
3. Overview of the building at night

2

3

2

With a diameter of 230 metres and cantilevering of 54 metres on each side of the stands, the roof is carried by 36 pairs of cables whose pre-tensioning is brought together via a circular double tension ring of strand-bundle cables above the pitch. Placed at various heights, the tension rings are linked together by 18-metre-high air supports, and together with the compression ring at the edge of the stadium producing a balance of forces on the principle of a spoked wheel.

1 Close-up of the façade
2. Exterior stairs

3

1. Overview of the pitch
2. Pitch with grand stands
3. Reception

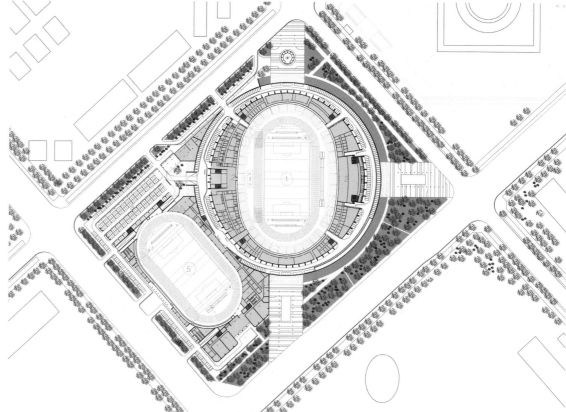

1. Pitch
2. Entrance areas
3. Stands and VIP boxes
4. Parking
5. Training field

Moses Mabhida Stadium

Designer: gmp - von Gerkan, Marg and Partners Architects **Location:** Durban, South Africa **Completion:** 2009 **Photographer:** Marcus Bredt **Site area:** 190,000 m²

The Moses Mabhida Stadium is situated on an elevated platform in the central sports park on the shore of the Indian Ocean, and is accessed from the city and station via a broad flight of steps. A 105-metre arch rises high over the stadium as a landmark that is visible from afar. The main entrance at the south end of the 1.5-kilometre long linear park symbolises the stadium's gateway to the city, and is formed by the bifurcation of the huge arch. At the north end, a cable car transports visitors to the "Skydeck" at the apex of the arch. From here, you get a panoramic view of the city and the Indian Ocean.

For the 2010 World Cup, the stadium was fitted with seating for 70,000 spectators. Afterwards, the number was reduced to 56,000, but can be temporarily increased to as many as 85,000 for major events. The multi-purpose stadium not only meets FIFA requirements but also can host the Commonwealth Games or Olympic Games. The building offers excellent conditions for participants, journalists and spectators, with VIP facilities, the President and Ocean Atriums – both over six storeys high – clubrooms and 130 spectator boxes.

The shape of the bowl results from the interaction of the circular roof structure with the triple-radius geometry of the arena. The great arch carries the weight of the inner membrane roof. The unusual geometry of the cable system is derived logically from the structure. The PTFE-coated roof membrane admits 50% of the sunlight into the arena while also providing shade.

The perforated façade membrane of profiled metal sheeting rises to the outer edge of the roof, forming a lively pattern of light and shadow and offering glimpses of the interior, which lends the stadium a light and airy feel.

Inspired by the typical palette of colours of Durban's coastal landscape, the designers chose a "maritime" colour scheme for the seat shells, ranging from blue and green to ivory, paling from dark at the bottom to light on the top rows. From a distance, the empty seats in different colours look already occupied, and make a cheerful sight.

The artificial lighting of the stadium is not just functional, but also serves to illuminate the architecture, floodlighting some parts and spotlighting or highlighting others. The roof surfaces on either side of the great arch are illuminated on top by a line of LEDs mounted directly on the arch. The rest of the roof membrane is lit from below by floodlights installed on the catwalk.

Awarded:
IABSE 2011 Outstanding Structure Awards, Finalist, 2011
German Light Design Price "International Project", 2011
Master Builders Association Excellence in Construction Awards Iconic Award, 2010
SAICE Durban Branch Award: Special Award for Excellence as Defining Project of the Decade, 2010
IMPUMELELO Innovation Awards: Sustainability Award for the Greening strategy, 2010

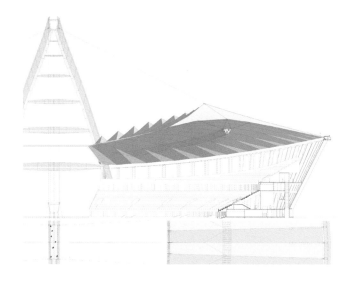

1. PTFE membrane
2. 1500 parking places
3. 130 boxes on two levels
4. 350m straddling steel arch with cable car
5. Third temporary tier made of steel

1. Aerial view
2. Overview of the building at daylight

1. Exterior view from entrance
2. Details of the arch
3. Side view at daylight

3

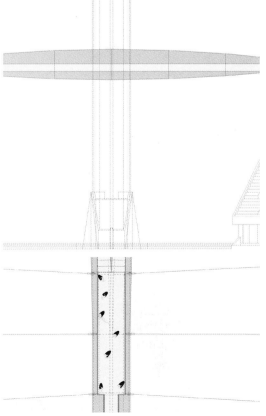

1 Main hall
2. Corridor
3. Lounge
4. View from inside hall to the stand

3

4

1. Overview of pitch
2. Side view of pitch
3, 4. Bottom of the auditorium
5. Ba throom

3

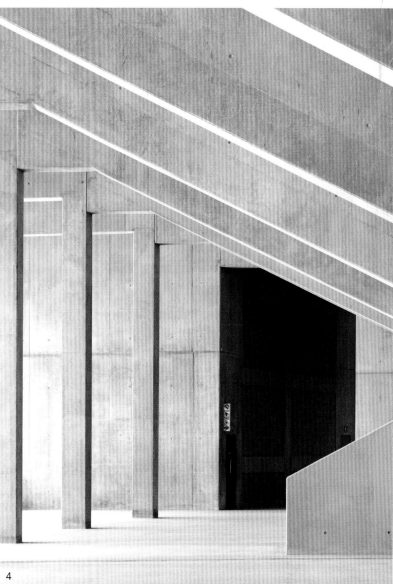

4

5

Cape Town Stadium

Designer: gmp - von Gerkan, Marg and Partners Architects **Location:** Cape Town, South Africa
Completion: 2009 **Photographer:** Marcus Bredt, Bruce Sutherland **Building area:** 110,000 m²

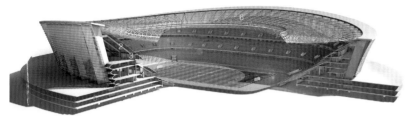

1. Perforated PTFE-membrane façade
2. Temporary upper tier
3. Upper circulating area
4. Lower circulating area
5. Parking
6. Suspension roof as tensile cable structure with
   upper glass covering and internal membrane

The image of Cape Town is uniquely characterised by the interaction of Table Mountain and Signal Hill, a soft, hilly landscape and the surrounding Atlantic Ocean.

Green Point Stadium is situated as a solitary body, embedded in Green Point Common at the foot of Signal Hill and is ordered respectfully into the landscaped complex.

The exterior shell of the stadium was designed as an abstract, linearly arranged membrane construction. Its unique undulating silhouette, which is the result of the geometry of the stadium body, transforms the stadium into a sculptural object and intensifies its integration into the existing landscape.

The light membrane is composed of expansive concave elements that form a cohesive flowing façade, which follows the stadium's undulating shape. The light-coloured glass-fiber tissue emphasizes this effect, since its colour creates a sense of depth and animation, and the translucent surface absorbs and reflects the effect of the existing daylight. At sunset, the stadium possesses a reddish glow, a blue one on a bright summer day and has a grey appearance on a stormy day in winter.

The stadium, designed to accommodate football and rugby games, provides seating for approximate 68,000 spectators, divided over three tiers. Of these seats, 1,800 are business seats and a further 1,500 are intended for VIP and press use. Thanks to their inclination, all seats possess excellent visibility of the field.

The interior of the stadium is designed in such a way that its entire focus is directed on the playing field, creating an intense and exciting atmosphere.

The roof construction is a combination of a suspended roof with radial truss structure. The undulating roof is outfitted with laminated safety glass elements and its interior is faced with a diaphanous membrane. Technical features are integrated into the space between the glass roofing and the membrane, such as acoustic and lighting systems. This space also provides protection from the weather and serves as a sound insulating volume.

The stadium, with its respectful reserve, is destined to become one of the city's landmark features. It will help to gentrify its direct surroundings around the Green Point Common and will function as an additional impetus for further positive developments in the adjoining urban structure, neighbourhood and the entire urban fabric.

Awarded:
2010 Consulting Engineers South Africa's (CESA) Glenrand MIB Engineering Excellence Awards, Commendation
2010 German Steel Construction Award
2011 IOC/IAKS Gold Medal

1. The sports area is designed to accommodate football and rugby games
2. The façades and underside of the roof are cladded in a translucent glass fabric with a silver coating
3. The Cape Town Stadium that lies to the seaside of Cape Town
4. The stadium's façade is designed as a horizontally profiled membrane

3

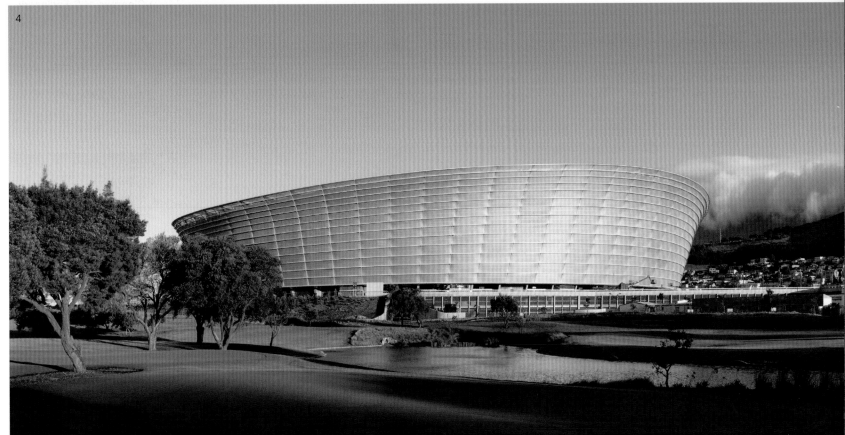

4

1. The stadium features a curved laminated glass roof
2. The auditorium provides seating for approximate 68,000 spectators, divided over three tiers
3. Entrance to the auditorium
4. Bottom of the auditorium

1. Playground
2. Auditorium
3. Athletes' entrance
4. Circulating area

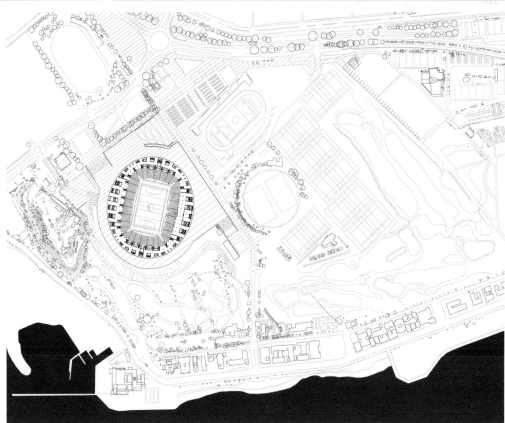

Astana Arena

Designer: Tabanlıoğlu Architects, Melkan Gürsel & Murat Tabanlıoğlu **Location:** Astana, Kazakhstan
Completion: 2009 **Photographer:** Cemal Emden **Site area:** 232,485 m² **Building Area:** 66,521 m²

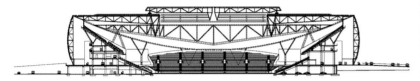

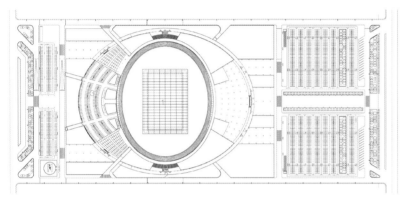

1. Main playground
2. Entrance
3. Grand stand

Apart from its functional features, the Astana Stadium is designed specifically for Astana City to be a symbolic building that reflects the modern and contemporary aspects of the new capital of Kazakhstan. Emerging from the vast landscape of Astana, located on the main road, which connects the city to the airport, the Stadium creates a symbolic link between people and country and Kazakhstan with the world.

The design introduces innovative solutions adopting high technology principles for operational management, interaction with the environment and especially with harsh climatic conditions of the geography. An operable roof system that functions independently from the fixed roof is programmed in order to protect the green area and provide eligible conditions for the spectators and players.

The stadium can be used for different sports and gathering purposes but it is mainly programmed as a soccer field, which will be covered with high quality artificial grass that fits the FIFA and UEFA criteria. In accordance with various needs the field will be covered with high-tech materials (i.e. pitch cover). The pitch area is (68 metres x 105 metres) 7,140 square metres.

Car parks and service roads for 1,411 cars are planned on 71,650 square metres, outside of these secure spaces where, in unison, the ticket offices are located. In addition to the parking capacity, a 9,000-square-metre VIP and media car park is secured behind the west wing.

The sliding roof is an integral part of the structure of the stadium. When it is closed, it converts the stadium into a covered arena; whether closed or open, the roof is an elementary part of the whole. The elliptical geometry reveals itself on the weatherproof roof shell. The main bearing construction of the roof is steel. The rectangular opening is as big as the soccer field.

Each spectator's platform has its separate stairways; the vertical scale of the facility, the positioning and the height of vertical transportation provide easier access to the roads around the stadium. The circulation is maintained by platforms on 5.50 level. Six separate zones, behind the different levels of the stand areas, are spared as concourse that open to food kiosks, restaurants and sufficient number of restrooms.

The stadium is conceived as a large fortress, which makes a distinctive and unmistakable impression both when it is seen from a distance and from close up; it will constitute a charming urban landscape and become a new scene in Astana.

Awarded:
Trimo Architectural Award 2009
International Property Award 2011

1. The exterior wall glazed in the daylight
2. Greenish exterior at night
3. The stadium is like a large fortress

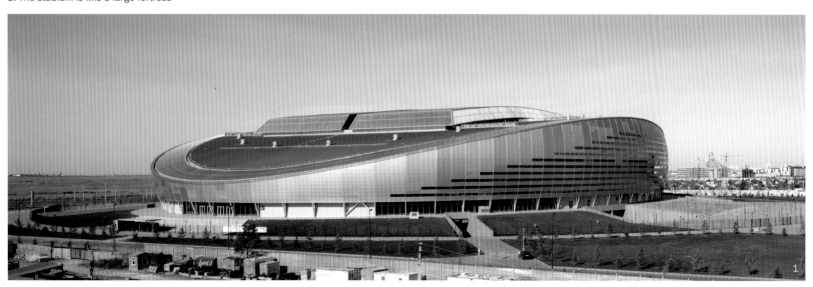

1. The entrance hall
2. The playing filed and stand with sliding roof

Metricon Stadium

Designer: Populous **Location:** Gold Coast, Australia **Completion:** 2011 **Photographer:** Scott Burrows
Site area: 12.7 Hectares **Building area:** 24,500 m²

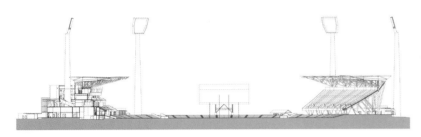

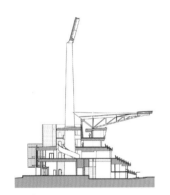

The new Metricon Stadium at Carrara, designed by Populous, is one of the best regional oval stadium in Australia, with a focus on flexibility and sustainability. Home to the new Gold Coast Football Club, the multi-use stadium is capable of hosting not only AFL but also Twenty-20 Cricket, international cricket and major outdoor concerts. The 25,000-seat stadium has also been designed to accommodate the requirements of the bid by the Gold Coast for the 2018 Commonwealth Games.

Metricon Stadium sets a new standard in environmentally sustainable design with the integration of a "solar halo" into the roof. This exciting concept establishes the stadium as a solar power generator with 20% of the stadiums power usage provided through photo-voltaic cells integrated into the "solar halo".

The stadium represents a unique development of the community stadium with the traditions of "footy in the park" developed to encourage family participation and enjoyment at the event. The new stadium has one of Australia's largest video boards providing a unique fan experience, which when combined with the open setting compliments and the outdoor life style of the Gold Coast.

New concepts of the stadium club, the field suite and open corporate barbeque terraces create new hospitality opportunities on the Coast as well as providing a unique fan experience at the stadium for all patrons. Public food courts are located in the park creating outdoor picnic and BBQ areas, which reinforce the park setting nature of the stadium. This new approach to the footy stadium is focused on families and the community and providing a truly unique Gold Coast experience.

The identity of Metricon Stadium and its uniqueness to the Gold Coast lifestyle is further reinforced by the roof design. The undulating wave-form roof is reminiscent of the swell of the Broadbeach Surf and the undulating backdrop of the hinterland. Colour is also used to give the stadium a sense of identity and to root it firmly as being of the Gold Coast – bright, fresh and young.

1. View to Stadium from Nerang-Broadbeach Road entry plaza
2. View to West Stand Entry Metricon Stadium
3. View to West Stand from field of play

2

3

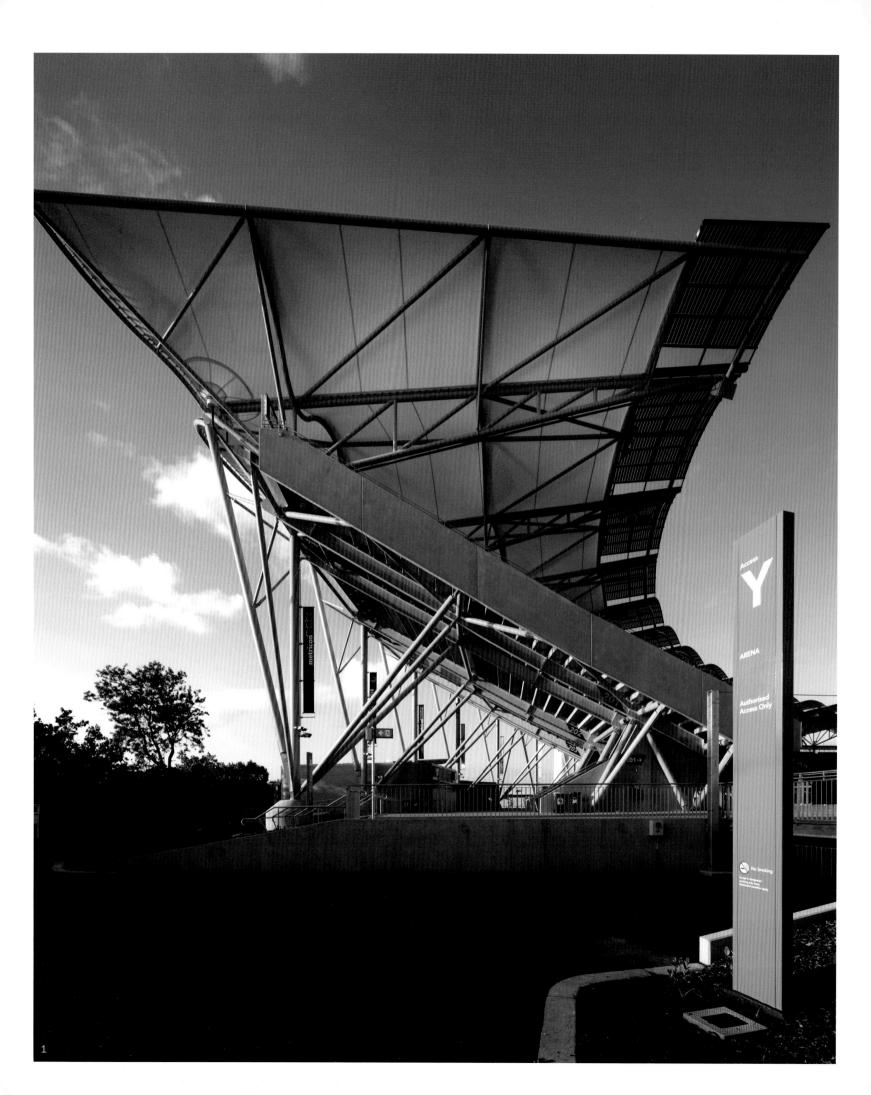

1. East stand upper tier seating
2. Pedestrian access from F&B outlets to east stand concourse
3. East stand concourse

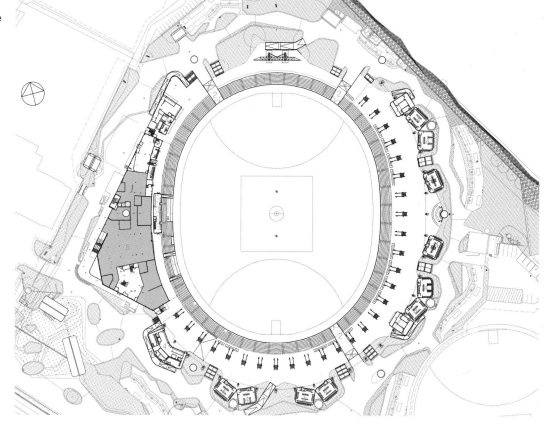

1. Auditorium
2. Athlete entrance
3. Platform
4. Toilet
5. Cafe

1. View from north stand
2. View from south stand upper seating tier
3. BBQ terrace
4. The deck

Wembley Stadium

Designer: Populous and Foster + Partners **Location:** London, UK **Completion:** 2007 **Photographer:** Nigel Young (Foster + partners), Hufton Crow **Site area:** 103,700 m²

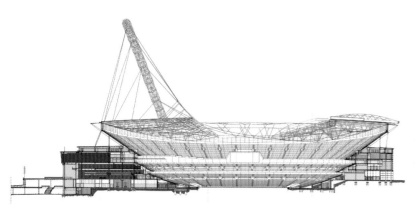

Throughout its 80-year history, the old Wembley Stadium was undoubtedly the most famous sporting and entertainment venue in Britain. The new 90,000 seats state-of-the-art Wembley Stadium, opened in 2007, has built upon its past heritage to become one of the world's most dynamic stadiums.

The visibly striking image of the 133-metre Wembley Stadium arch, piercing the London skyline, not only provides the city of London with an iconic landmark, it also holds a crucial function in supporting the 7,000 tonne steel roof structure, eliminating the need for pillars. Replacing the twin towers, the white steel arch, the longest single roof structure in the world, was developed from Rod Sheard's earlier work in Sydney on the main stadium for the 2000 Olympic Games.

Wembley, which is also the English National Stadium, is one of the largest stadium buildings in the world: a kilometre around the circumference. The technological advances, top quality fittings and finishings, and range of conference facilities and restaurants all help to create depth and diversity to maximise revenue streams and ensure the building is used as much as possible. There are 5,500 premium dining seats in four of the biggest restaurants in London, supplemented by 150 private suites, a Royal Lounge for 400 and The Great Hall that can seat 1,000. On a non-match day each of the large function areas can operate independently of one another. Rigging points for dressing the stadium and function rooms to the users' needs are located within the ceiling and on the walls in the central atrium. The façade glazing system can take large banners cloaking the stadium. Effectively, the design intent was to create a blank canvas, which allowed event owners to "dress" and theme the space or whole building, both inside and out, to reflect their event. The neutrality is based on hard, durable finishes in a palette of white and graduated greys, and the dressing uses colour in textiles, banners, and lighting. The arch is a series of interlocking sections designed in a diamond latticework, giving a light weight appearance but in reality functioning to support the roof structure. By using the arch to bear some of the weight of the roof, it has enabled a series of retractable panels to be installed over the southern stand. This lets light and air onto the pitch, allowing the turf to grow as naturally as possible, thus maintaining a pitch similar in quality to the old stadium. Between events the roof is left open, but can be moved to cover all the seats within 15 minutes, ensuring fans are sheltered during an event.

The geometry of the seating bowl, designed as a single bowl, rather than four separate stands, increases the intensity, and atmosphere, ensuring all 90,000 spectators have an unobstructed view. Some of the special features of the old stadium have also been incorporated in the new design, including the east-west orientation and the presentation route.

Although designed primarily for rugby, football and concerts, the new stadium is capable of hosting world-class athletics events by means of a platform adaption.

1,2. Wembley arch aerial, and the arch also functions to support the roof structure eliminating the need for pillars
3,4. The visibly striking image of the 133-metre Wembley Stadium arch

3

4

1. Wembley roof
2. Ground view
3. Nightshot

2

1. Wembley concourse. The interiors are deliberately neutral in colour, based on hard durable finishes in a paletter of white and graduated greys to provide a "blank canvas" allowing event owners to "dress" the particular space
2. Wembley interiors

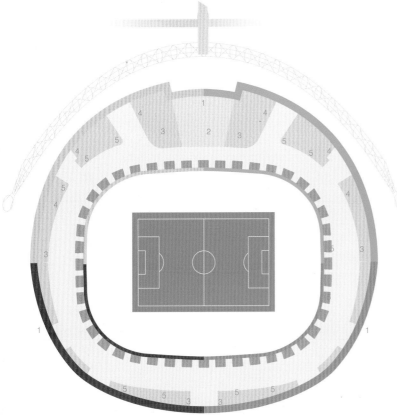

1. Club Wembley north entrance – level 1
2. Bobby Moore room
3. First aid
4. Information point
5. Bar

Forsyth Barr Stadium, Dunedin

Designer: Populous, in cooperation with Jasmax **Location:** Dunedin, New Zealand **Completion:** 2011
Photographer: Populous, Marina Matthews **Site area:** 5.56ha **Building area:** 27,200 m²

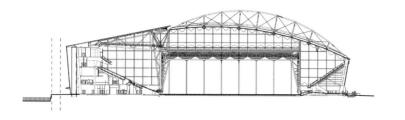

Populous is engaged to design the new multi-purpose stadium in Dunedin, New Zealand to replace the legendary Carisbrook House of Pain. The rectangular stadium incorporates a flexible seating arrangement, which provides 20,000 permanent seats, 5,000 re-locatable seats and 5,000 student reserves all located under a transparent fixed roof that also covers the field. The revolutionary design provides a natural turf playing field growing under a fixed roof, a feature that has been made possible by advances in roofing and material technology.

The stadium is located at the southern end of the South Island in New Zealand at latitude 42˚ south, the most southerly professional stadium in the world. The stadium is subject to extreme weather events making the roof an essential feature of the stadium to encourage crowds to attend live events.

The unique roof and cladding design is the result of extensive research by the design team. The sectional profile of the stadium has been carefully designed to maximise the solar penetration onto the field as well as the natural ventilation of the playing surface to create the optimum condition for turf growth under a roof. The roof and façades are cladded in ETFE, which is the first time the true technical qualities of this revolutionary material have been used in a stadium.

The stadium is being master planned to create a truly urban stadium. The University of Otago is to be integrated into the western end of the ground and a flexible exhibition/event space is also being planned creating an entertainment and cultural heart for the city.

1. The ETFE roof and façades have been designed to maximise the amount of sunlight on the natural pitch
2. View of the stadium from Logan Park
3. Large openings around the base of the building allow the field to be naturally ventilated

1. Forsyth Barr Stadium is located at the edge of Dunedin's city centre, between the harbour and the University precinct
2,3. Views of the South and East Stands from across Otago Harbour

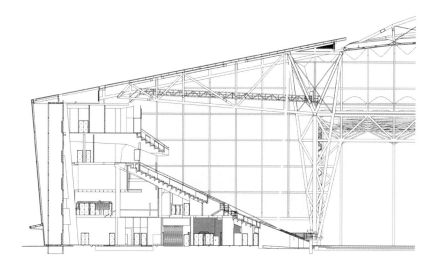
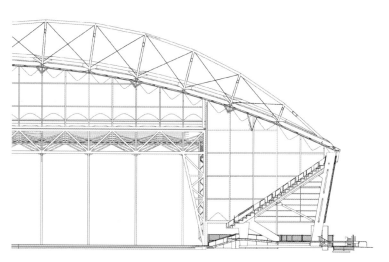

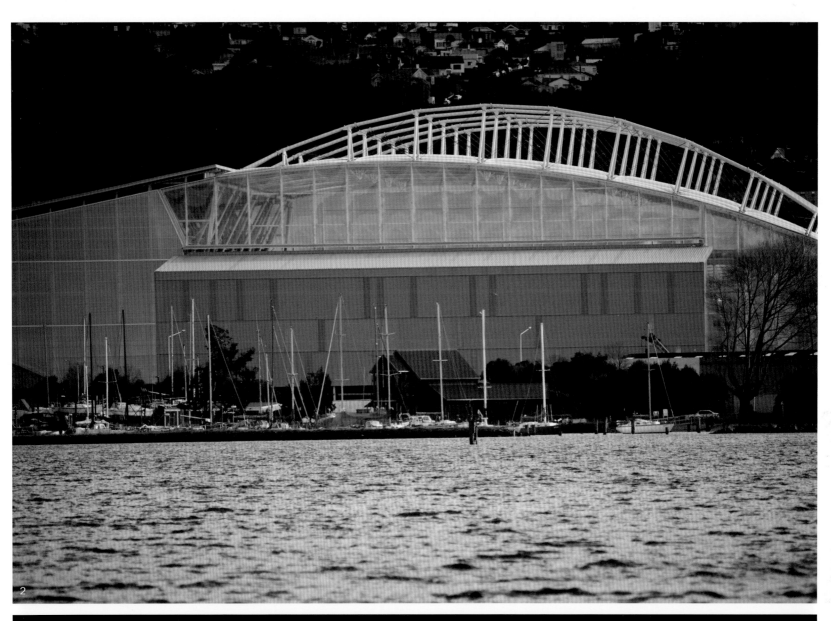

1. The natural pitch was sown in January 2011 and successfully sustained four Rugby World Cup matches played here in September and October
2. View from the South Stand

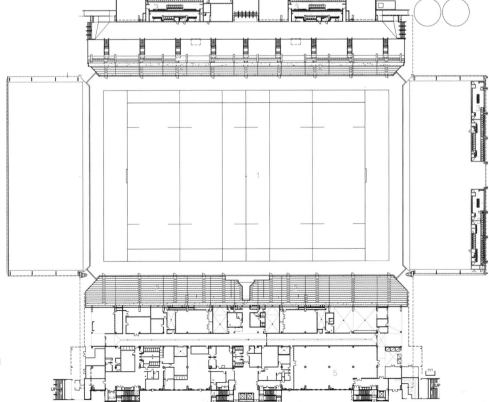

1. Filed of play
2. Seating bowl
3. Restrooms
4. Staircase
5. Kitchen

Universiade 2011 Sports Centre

Designer: gmp - von Gerkan, Marg and Partners Architects **Chinese partner practices:** SADI, CNADRI, CCDI, BLY **Location:** Shenzhen, China **Completion:** 2011 **Photographer:** Christian Gahl **Building area:** 870,000 m²

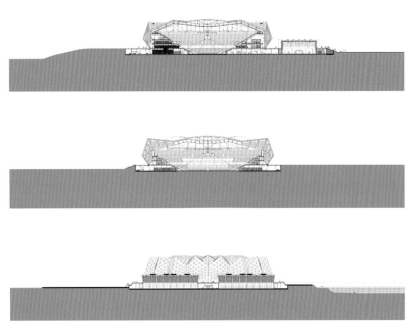

The Universiade Sports Centre has to satisfy the functional requirements of both international sports events and the organisation of other smaller and larger-scale events and concerts. The objective is to create a culturally significant, symbolic project for Shenzhen.

The design is inspired by the surrounding undulating landscape. This enables topographical modulation in the sports centre area, with flows of people on various levels. An artificial lake connects the stadium at the foot of the mountain with the circular multifunctional hall in the north and the rectangular swimming hall west thereof. The central plaza is accessed via a raised promenade from the individual stadia.

The overall complex is laid out as an extensive landscaped park with typical elements of a traditional Chinese garden. Watercourses and plants symbolise movement and development, while crystalline structures in the form of stones and rocks represent continuity and stability. The dialogue between the fluid landscape shapes and the expressive architecture of the stadia constitutes the conceptual framework of the design. The crystalline shape of the three stadia is additionally emphasized by the illumination of the translucent façades at night.

The stadium is planned to be multifunctional, meeting the requirements of local, national and international sports occasions and events. Total capacity is 60,000, seated in three stands. The middle tier on the western side includes a 200-seat VIP stand with attached dignitaries' boxes. Between the middle and upper tier there are 60 VIP boxes with their associated seating.

All technical facilities required by participants and other functional areas are accommodated at field level beneath the stands. Guests of honour and media representatives can meet up here in the socialising zone provided. Access routes for individual user groups do not conflict.

The sports plaza serves as the main access level for spectators. Access to the lower tier and steps to the middle and upper tiers alternate with kiosks and sanitary facilities. The broad passageways allow attractive glimpses into the circular shape of the stadium from afar, and make for easy orientation. The curved upper tier is accessed via twelve broad staircases leading off the circulating area, which allow impressive glimpses of the roof structure and the other stadia. The upper tier is divided into two parts, and as it is almost a circle, is doubly curved. In this way, the stadium has an exciting shape both on the inside and seen from outside.

The roof structure projects up to 65 metres, and is designed as a steel prismatic shell on a basis of triangular facets. The total diameter of the roof is 310 metres lengthways and 290 metres across. Both roof and façade have three layers each. The external façade layer is translucent glazing made up of triangular laminated safety glass panes or polycarbonate slabs. The interior membrane layer, likewise translucent, fulfils the requirements for shade and acoustics, and acts as a reflecting surface for the façade illumination. The folded primary and secondary steel structure is located in between. The major part of the technical installations is also integrated into this area.

The indoor sports complex is designed as a circular multifunctional arena for indoor sports competitions as well as for ice-skating, mega-performances,

1. Panorama view at night
2. Bird view of the stadium in the daytime
3. Close-up of the façade

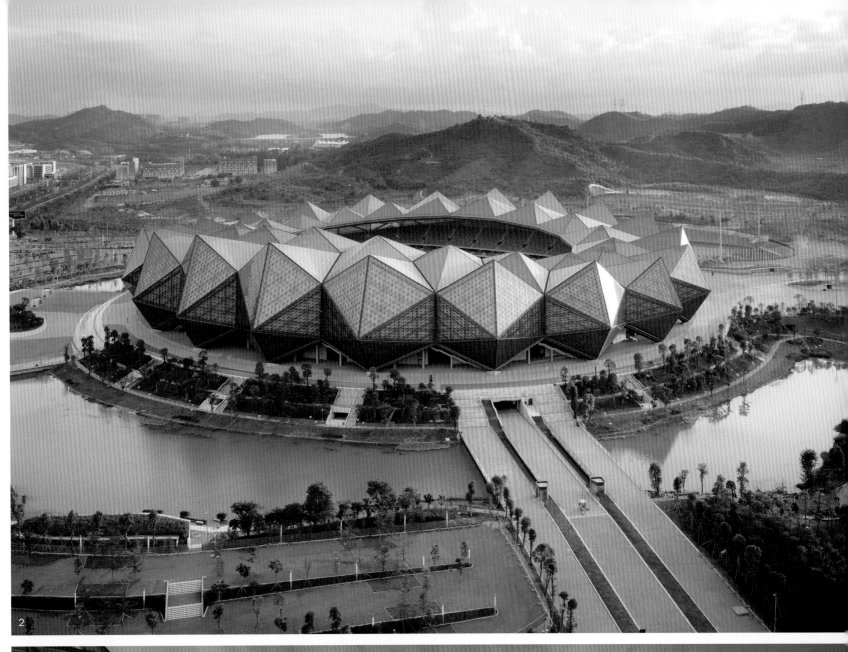

1

social gathering and small-scale exhibition shows. The overall capacity is approx. 18,000 spectators. The seats are arranged on two stands, the first rows of the lower stand with a total number of 3,000 seats are movable. The seating organisation is laid out for optimal viewing as well as for even circulation and distribution of the people. The arena offers supreme viewing conditions in all areas.

The swimming complex forms the third important module of the Shenzhen Universiade Sports Centre. Its architectural design takes into account the functional requirements of this type of building as well the overall architectural appearance of the crystalline volumes in the park. The overall capacity is approx. 3,000 spectators, the seats are arranged on two stands. The swimming complex is clearly divided into a competition and a leisure swimming area.

1. Night view of the stadium's façade
2. Swimming hall
3. Interior translucent membrane layer

1

1. Pitch
2. Arena

1. Plaza
2. Outdoor arena
3. Swimming pool
4. Main sports complex
5. Warm-up arena
6. Main sports stadium
7. Sports central plaza

Shanghai Oriental Sports Centre

Designer: gmp - von Gerkan, Marg and Partners Architects **Location:** Shanghai, China **Completion:** 2011 **Photographer:** Marcus Bredt **Site area:** 34.75 hectares **Building area:** 163,800 m²

The Oriental Sports Centre (SOSC) was built on the occasion of the 14th FINA World Swimming Championships in Shanghai. The sports complex was designed and built by architects von Gerkan, Marg and Partners (gmp). It consists of a hall stadium for several sports and cultural events, a natatorium, an outdoor swimming pool and a media centre.

Water is the overarching theme of both the park and the architecture of the stadiums and the media centre. It is the connecting element between the buildings, which stand on raised platforms in specially constructed lakes. Thus the round stadiums have a curved lakeside shore round them, while the rectangular natatorium has a straight lakeside shore. Design affinities and a shared formal idiom, and use of materials give the three stadiums structural unity. The steel structures of broad arches with large-format triangular elements are made of coated aluminum sheet form double-sided curved surfaces along the frame of the sub-structures, thus evoking sails in the wind.

Hall stadium: The hall has a crowd-capacity of 14,000, which can be increased to 18,000 by the use of mobile seating. The main structure of the closed building with a round ground plan consists of reinforced concrete, while the roof is a steel structure with a 170-metre span with aluminum cladding. The parallel steel girders create 35-metre-high arcades and include the glass façades of the encircling open foyer.

Natatorium: The natatorium contains four pools arrayed in a row: two standard-sized, one for diving and a leisure pool. It has over 3,500 fixed seats, which will be expanded to 5,000 for the world championships, to meet FINA requirements.

The swimming hall is a closed building with a rectangular ground plan, a main structure of reinforced concrete and a roof structure of sectional steel girders. The roof structure with triangular glass surfaces is around 210 metres long, 120 metres wide and 22 metres high. Direct, intrusive sunlight is forestalled by means of narrow top lights along the beams, without preventing natural day lighting.

Outdoor pool: This swimming complex is located in the open on an artificial island and offers 2,000 fixed stadium seats. For the World Swimming Championships and other outstanding events, capacity will be increased to 5,000 seats. The competition-size diving pool and diving towers are complemented by a competition pool. As in the other stadiums, the roof structure with its external diameter of 130 metres reflects the round ground-plan of the shell of the building. The inner diameter is around 90 metres. The roof trusses are carried by the building structure. A lightweight membrane between the modules provides protection against sun and rain.

Media centre: The 80-metre high high-rise building is on the northern side of the sports complex. Its 15 floors include a fitness centre, conference rooms and medical care centre, plus VIP and office areas. Because of the even 8.4 metres grid, the building can be used flexibly. With its external shell of white, perforated aluminum panels, the building interprets the undulating shape of the adjacent lake.

1. Distant view of the SOSC
2. Outdoor pool exterior
3. Natatorium exterior

1

1

2

1. Hall stadium
2. Hall stadium with plaza
3. Outdoor pool interior

3

1. Open pool
2. Natatorium
3. Gymnasium
4. Media centre

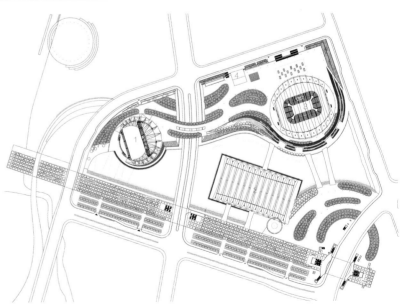

1

1. Natatorium interior
2. Standard pool in the natatorium

2

Gobela Sports Complex

Designer: Ander Marquet Ryan, JAAM architects **Location:** Bizkaia, Spain **Completion:** 2008
Photographer: JAAM architects **Site area:** 31,983 m²

The programme Gobela Sports Complex is situated in the town of Getxo, the city of Bizkaia, Spain and has a surface area of 15,088 square metres. The application of this programme needs a floor area of 31,983 square metres and the building area exhausts to make the plot boundary perimeter to be built.

This programme is organised into three main areas:

Football field, bleachers for 1,300 spectators, shops and underground parking with a capacity of less than 300 seats.

Sports hall for 360 spectators, bar and cafe (shared with soccer field) and offices for local clubs.

Sports field: swimming pools (a swimming pool, a training pool for swimming, a splash pool of swimming and a regulatory pool for swimming of 25 metres), two tennis courts, two paddle courts, multipurpose rooms (fitness, aerobics, martial arts, gym, dance room and psychomotor) and the administration offices.

The aim was to take the irregular boundary of a parcel as a border built to solve formal and constructive drive a large container with different geometries sports facilities: swimming pools, soccer fields, tenniscourts, paddle tenniscourts, sports halls, offices...

The result is arranged in a common skin, of white concrete corrugated panels, resolved by seeking a rhythm in the concrete enclosure without affecting their unity while relieving their large size.

The silhouette formed by the corrugated panels cladding breaks, ebbs and adapting to the needs of the programme. In its interior play areas inside and outside walls are separated by perforated steel or transparent polycarbonate that draw between all equipment accessories.

For the realisation of the panels were designed five molds with different undulations but with identical ends flush. The aim was to provide a rhythm to the concrete enclosure without affecting its unity and to ease its large dimensions. Finally, for budgetary reasons the number of molds is reduced to two.

1. Football field & tennis courts
2. The building is surrounded by water features
3. White wall of the building is glazed at daylight

1 Tennis court
2. Façade

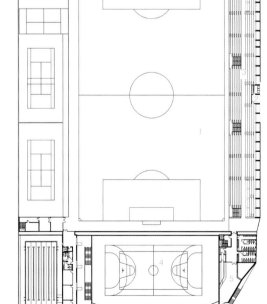

1. Football field
2. Football pressroom
3. Audience
4. Basketball court
5. Café
6. Swimming
7. Administration office

2

1. The football field with grand stand
2. Swimming pools
3. Basketball court
4. Floor of the corridor shining with light

Bilbao Arena and Sports Centre

Designer: Javier Perez Uribarri and Nicolás Espinosa Barrientos (ACXT Architects) **Location:** Bilbao, Spain **Completion:** 2010 **Photographer:** Aitor Ortiz, (c) ACXT IDOM **Building area:** 30,685m²

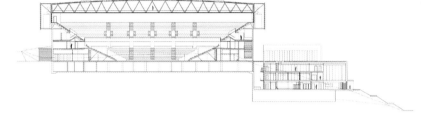

The building is divided into two clearly differentiated volumes: the largest one plays to look like a forest, which would melt into the surrounding park; while the lower volume operates like the rock anchoring the upper volume.

The programme is divided between both volumes: the largest, the forest, comprises a competition court for basketball and indoor soccer with a maximum capacity for 8,500 spectators; the smallest, the rock, comprises a 25-metre swimming pool with 6 lanes; 3 gymnasiums, and management offices. A parking site for 240 vehicles has been planned under the competition track.

The pavilion is much more than the seat of Bilbao Basket. It has a multipurpose court, three gymnasiums, a swimming pool and parking site for over 200 vehicles. The pool is 25 metres and is covered with green crystals, plenty of natural light and views of the top level clubs.

All levels of the building have direct access to the outside.

The gym is equipped with the latest technology. It has 73 exercise machines, including cardio machines, bicycles, stepping machines and weight benches, traditional levers and so on. It also has a virtual coach, television screen and USB connection to load up the iPod while playing a little exercise.

The district already has Miribilla new sports facilities. The Palace of Sports has brought to the locals a sports and entertainment centre, which is capable of hosting large concerts.

1. View at night
2. Building façade
3. Green wall shining with sunlight

1

2

3

3

1. Swimming pool
2. Fitness centre
3. Multipurpose hall

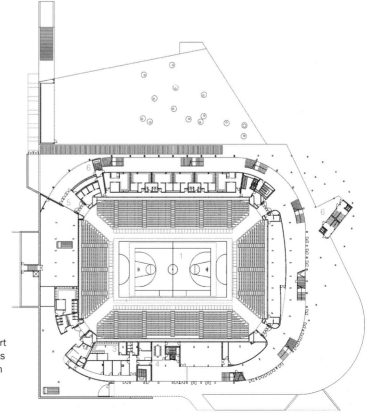

1. Basketball court
2. Spectator seats
3. Changing room
4. Meeting room
5. Entrance
6. Stairs

1

1 Passageway
2. Entrance and stairs
3. Basketball court with huge stand around
4. Basketball court at interior light

Arena Zagreb

Designer: UPI-2M **Location:** Zagreb, Croatia **Completion:** 2008 **Photographer:** Robert Les, Milienko Hegedic, Vanja Solin, UPI-2M **Building area:** 90,340m²

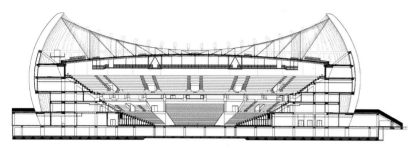

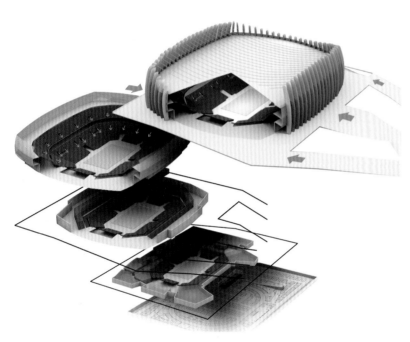

Arena Zagreb is the multipurpose indoor arena located in Zagreb, Croatia, and it's built as a central sports hall for hosting the 2009 World Men's Handball Championship.

Arena Zagreb has been designed as multifunctional hall with all spatial and functional characteristics that enable maximal flexibility and provide realisation of various events. That is mostly achieved by flexibility of the grandstand, then preserving sufficient and various spaces reserved for athletes, other performers and event managers, by providing simple and fluid visitors circulation from entering point to the seats on the stand and offer various catering facilities, dividing the whole building in smaller mutually independent spatial zones that can be used separately, then acoustic interventions inside the hall shell and at last in securing sufficient bearing capacity of steel roof structure, capable for suspension of additional scene equipment.

Arena Zagreb is positioned at one of the city's main high-way entrances, in visual axis of one of the main city roads and axis of popular city recreation zone - Jarun Lake. Local surroundings are area of currently huge shopping and residential development.

Functional area partition follows the circulation routes of different users. All zones are mutually independent and equipped with sufficient number of separated accesses with very clear user's circulation system - quick and easy entering and exiting is secured, and mixing user's circulation routes are avoided. The unique shape of this building is strongly inspired by its significance in the city context, but also by its mega-structural characteristics that predefined main bearing elements - 86 large pre-stressed, pre-fabricated concrete curved columns form the main façade, mutually connected by translucent polycarbonate envelope.

The size of such venues, in comparison with the standard city scale, also implicates the significance they have in the global city image.

By fine designed shaping synergized with structural requirements and urban context, all conditions are fulfilled for iconic recognition and for access to the list of city emblems.

Awarded:

Innovation and Design Awards' Finalist by Conde Nast Traveller Magazine, 2010
Award for Structural Design of the Year at WAF, 2009
World Architecture Festival Finalist, Sports Category, 2009
Finalist for ARCHDAILY Awards for the Best Sports Building 2010 - 2011
Finalist for ARHITEKTON Magazine Year Award 2011 – 2011

1. People walking by the lake could enjoy a great view of the building
2. The arena is located beside the Jarun Lake
3. Bird view of the building

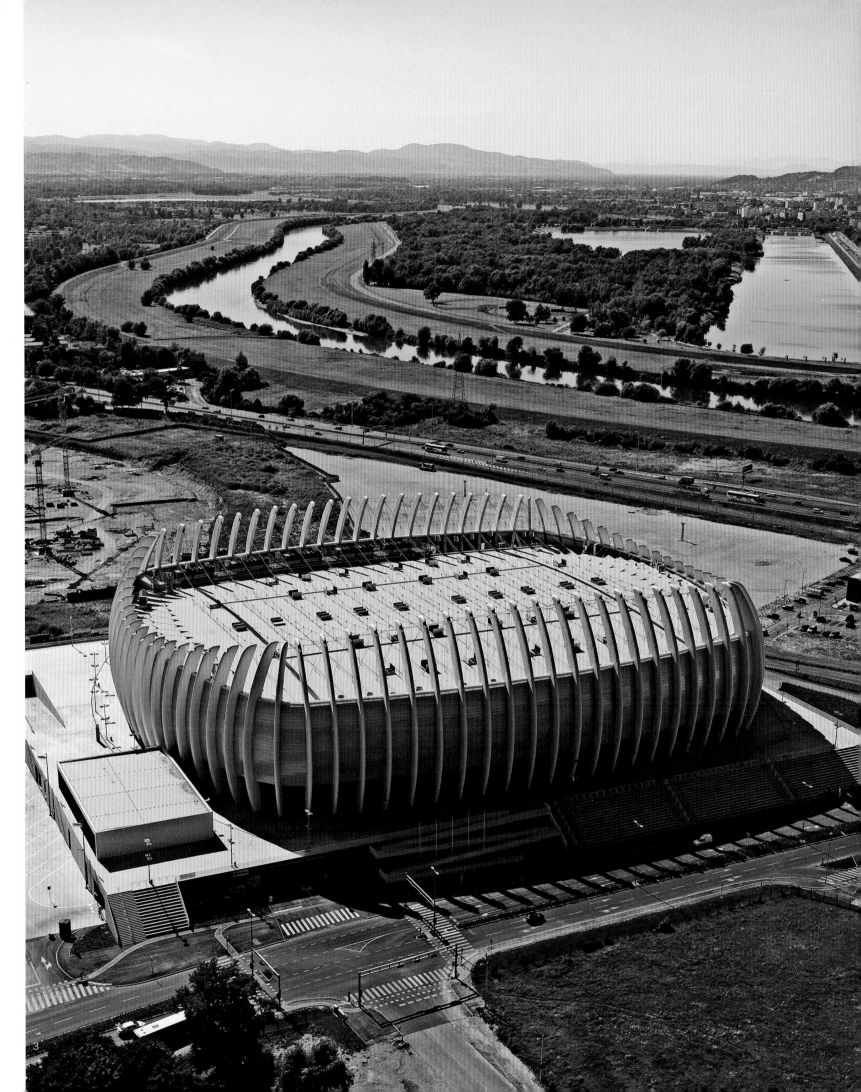

1. Arena Zagreb façade
2. Arena Zagreb glazed with light
3. Indoor arena

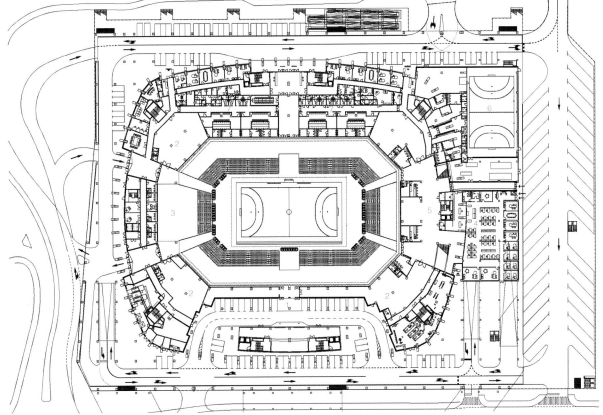

1. VIP entrance
2. Technical
3. Performance
4. Offices
5. Café
6. Training gym
7. Athletes management

Coliseums for South American Games

Designer: Giancarlo Mazzanti & Felipe Mesa **Location:** Medellin, Colombia **Completion:** 2009
Photographer: Giancarlo Mazzanti & Felipe Mesa **Building area:** 30,694m²

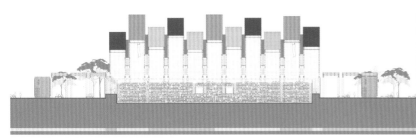

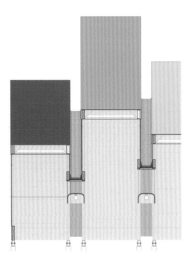

The project has been thought as a new geography to the interior of the elongated Aburrá Valley, midway between Cerro Nutibara and Cerro El Volador. It is a building that seems to be another mountain in the city; from the remote or from the top has an abstract image geographic and festive; from the inside, the movement of the steel structure, allows the filtered sunlight to get inside of the space, which is the suitable condition for the conduct of sporting events.

This project took the interior and exterior in a unified way. The outdoor public space and sporting venues are in a continuous space, thanks to a large deck built through extensive stripes out, perpendicular to the direction of the positioning of the main buildings. Each of the four sporting venues operates independently, but in terms of urban space behaves as one large continent built with public open spaces, semi-covered public spaces, and indoor sports. This project has three possible groups:

Each of the four scenarios can be understood as a separate building, which is connected with another on an urban scale. The three new scenarios can also be understood as a single large building, related to the existing Ivan de Bedout Coliseum. The four coliseums can be understood as a great place to set both the buildings and public space.

1. The skeleton of the project is the pattern.

Here the structure is an organisation system or the understanding of vitality. It means that the relation of the project proposing is its skeleton.

2. The skeleton of the project is made of the symmetry of the structure and the muscles.

Here the structure is the way in which the limit or physiognomy of the project are equivalent to the skeleton. The skeleton is on the outside or the epidermis and vice versa, and it is an expression of architecture. Architecture is qualified by the structure.

3. The skeleton of the project is the structure.

Columns, bases, beams, roofs; stripes, canals; interior space

In the interior of the sceneries the image of the skeleton seems raw when the trusses are exposed, they are no longer melted down with the skin but directly with the structure. The force lines loose a little of vigour due to its swelling and the perception of a hat becomes more evident, even the industrial image. The project melts public space with the interior activities because the structure avoids finishing (stopping) at the swelling. The skeleton of this project is a real structure.

1. Façade
2. The sports building with outdoor arena filed
3. Bird view of the whole sports space

1. Indoor arena court with grand stands
2. Corridor
3. Indoor arena court

1. Weightlifting competition zone
2. Weight men WC
3. Weight women WC
4. Disabled WC
5. Tables of judges and referees
6. Public toilets
7. Central competition
8. Heating zone
9. Cafeteria
10. Judges and coaches toilets
11. Multiple room
12. Sport goods stores
13. Female athletes WC
14. Female athletes backstage
15. Male athletes backstage
16. Male athletes WC
17. Nursing
18. Weighing area
19. Sauna

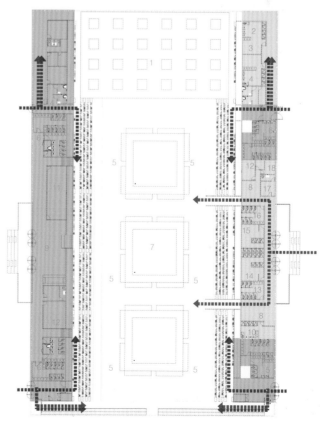

The Joan Gamper Training Facility for FC Barcelona

Designer: Enric Batlle & Joan Roig - BATLLE I ROIG ARQUITECTES **Location:** Barcelona, Spain
Completion: 2007 **Photographer:** Eva Serrats **Building area:** 135,000m²

The Joan Gamper training facility project for Football Club Barcelona, in the municipality of Sant Joan Despí, is a particularly important intervention for the promotion of sport in Catalonia.

The project has been developed slowly over recent years, materialising the club's old dream of bringing together its technical and sporting activities for professionals and amateurs in one place. This ranges from installations for training the first and the second football teams, for grassroots football and for basketball, handball and hockey.

The sports complex covers approximately 20 hectares, of which 13.5 hectares are given over to sport and the rest to road infrastructures and green areas. The training facility is laid out on two different levels to distinguish the first team and grassroots training pitches. The design included a series of buildings to serve various sporting activities, which are laid out around the edge of the complex in accordance with the function of each activity.

According to this criterion, the arrangement includes a sports block, a building with changing rooms for the first team, an office and service building, changing rooms for the grassroots football squad and a residence for sportsmen and women. The main buildings were designed with a unitary approach, with a single roof that accommodates them all and presents the main entrance to the complex via a large porch.

The Joan Gamper training facility consists of environmentally sustainable installations and is capable of producing at least the amount of energy it needs to run. It shows off its energy collectors by arranging them vertically on a tower that is designed as a landmark, presenting a point of reference and the image of the Club.

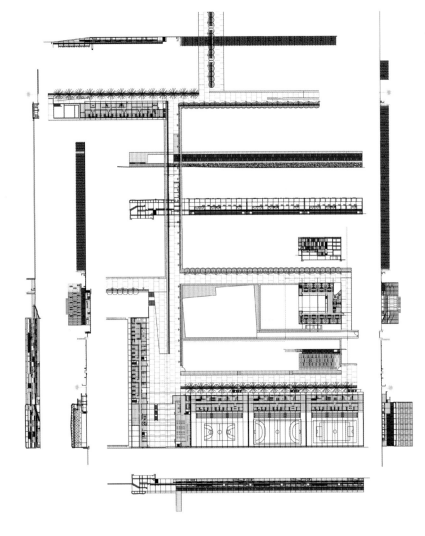

1. Side view of the building
2. Grass filed next to the building
3. Solid structure of the building

3

1. The building at night
2. Building, stand, integrated with grass field
3. Light shining at night

1. Training field
2. Lavatory
3. Meeting room
4. Changing room
5. Office
6. Washing room

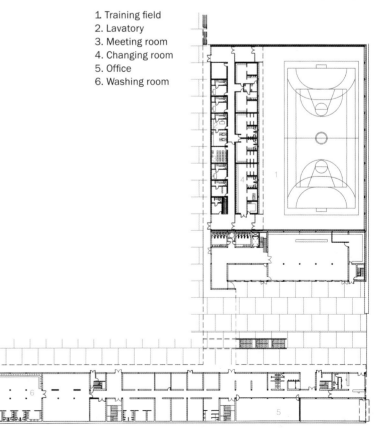

Soccer Stadium Nueva Balastera

Designer: Francisco José Mangado Beloqui **Location:** Palencia, Spain **Completion:** 2007 **Photographer:** Roland Halbe **Site area:** 15,200 m²

A soccer field has a fundamental and obvious function: to play soccer. But it also has two more functions that are not so evident but no less important. The first has to do with representation. A soccer field has become a work with certain iconic potential for the city. It can be a landmark, a building that is important not only for its quantitative characteristics, but also for its qualitative ones, a container for the dreams of the people. The second aspect stems from an obvious question: an area with the dimensions of a soccer field takes up a great expanse, which is used only on occasion. Doesn't this result in a waste of space? The answer is clearly yes.

The basic idea of this proposal rests on the belief that a soccer stadium is more of a building than an element of infrastructure. It is a building that can be taken advantage of to house other uses, but that above all, can and should recuperate a civil role. The project proposes perimeter offices and other public uses on the ground floor, all designed as a great urban "showcase" with direct and immediate access from the street. Internally the stadium is a large "surprise void" where in addition to soccer games, a variety of public spectacles can be enjoyed.

The residential setting in which the work is sited almost obliges one to recognise its condition and propose an urban building. The great scale of the building is derived from a structural language hidden by the perimeter, a perforated aluminium cladding that in addition to creating a rich dialogue of views between inside and outside. This skin fulfils the challenge of transforming the stadium into a city building, in spite of large-size achieves integration with its context.

The towers, necessary to illuminate the field, have the most symbolic roles. Lit, like large minerals with sculptural qualities, these towers can be seen from several kilometers away, establishing a dialogue in the landscape with Palencia's Cathedral. The designers are committing to the concept of stadium as urban building, without abandoning its festive character.

The soccer stadium is specific both conceptually and functionally. The public entrances are directly accessible from the street. The grand, gently sloping ramps are located at the corners and become the main entrances. The rest is organised along the perimeter in compliance with requirements for rapid evacuation. A system of parallel circulations function in parallel, and are superimposed, to allow the stadium's various uses to function independently of one another, the sporting functions and the offices.

Awarded:
First prize, Saloni Architectural Awards 2007

1. Exterior view of the building
2. Building façade

Nuevo Estadio Municipal La Balastera

1. Playing field
2. Staircase under seating
3. Corridor

1. Playing field
2. Audience zone
3. Stairs
4. Player's entrance (+.040m)
5. Washing room
6. Storehouse

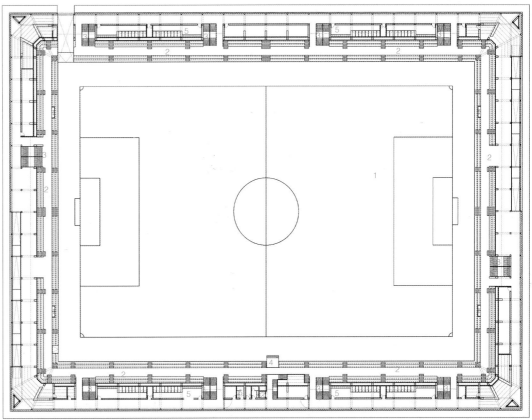

Carnegie Pavilion

Designer: ALSOP SPARCH **Location:** Leeds, UK **Completion:** 2010 **Photographer:** Christian Richters
Building area: 4,000 m²

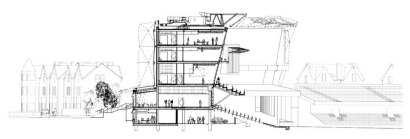

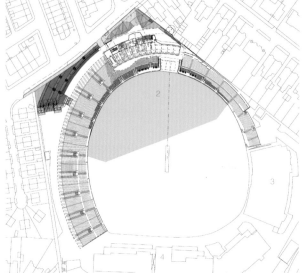

1. Carnegie Pavilion
2. Centre wicket axis
3. Carnegie stand
4. Rugby stand

The Carnegie Pavilion is a unique "dual-use" higher education and sports facility that will be occupied all year round. It is at one and the same time: a university faculty expanding beyond the campus and embedding itself within the surrounding community, within a working sports ground, and sports facility housing applied higher education – a "new paradigm in learning".

Leeds Metropolitan University entered into a unique partnership with Yorkshire County Cricket Club (YCCC) – supported by Yorkshire Forward – to not only enable the delivery of the Carnegie Pavilion, but also to provide mutual benefits for both organisations, enhancing higher education, sport and the all round sustainability of the development.

The Carnegie Pavilion will accommodate Leeds Met's School of Tourism, Hospitality and Events (THE), where students will benefit from direct exposure to real life sporting events and hospitality. The development incorporates a full-scale teaching kitchen as well as lecture theatres and faculty offices. Students of digital journalism will also be based in the building, and will work hands on with the hi-tech facilities of the new media centre, designed to meet the latest standards for both TV and radio broadcasting. The dual-use 150-seat auditorium for example, on major match days, converts into a 100-seat press box for cricket journalists, with uninterrupted views of the cricket action.

Co-occupation of the building (over 70% of the rooms have been designed for "dual-use") dramatically reduces its running costs, as well as its carbon footprint, when compared with two separate buildings. Indeed, the Carnegie Pavilion has achieved BREEAM "Excellent" standard whilst complying with ECB cricketing requirements including the south facing glazed wall providing uninterrupted sightlines.

Awarded:

BREEAM Code for "Excellent" Sustainable Buildings 2010
BREEAM (BRE Environmental Assessment Method) is the leading and most widely used environmental assessment method for buildings. It sets the standard for best practice in sustainable design and has become the de facto measure used to describe a building's environmental performance.

1. Roof structure
2. Stairs
3. Façade
4. The building with crystal-like exterior wall

1. There are grand stands below the building
2. The building is located next to the street
3. Details of the building wall
4. Glass wall shining at sunlight

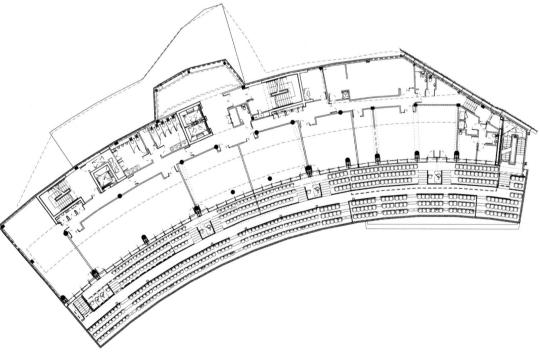

1

1. The media centre
2. View of the playing court from windows
3. Learning space

Sports Hall - FK Austria Wien Training Academy

Designer: Franz zt gmbh, atelier mauch gmbh **Location:** Vienna, Austria **Completion:** 2010
Photographer: Stephan Wyckoff **Site area:** 34,000 m² **Building area:** 2,630 m²

The academy training grounds of the junior teams of Austria Vienna - one of the most traditional football clubs in Austria - lies close to the "Franz Horr Stadium". They include a training hall and three grass pitches. The construction budget was extremely tight and the construction time was limited to six months, with a strict handover date after completion requirement in order to obtain the license of the Austrian Football League. Vienna building regulations set a maximum building height of 4.5 metres, so the 7.0 metres required clearance height in the training hall created an inevitable consequence: the entire building had to be lowered half below ground.

To assist the long-term refinancing of the construction budget, the principle of a football-advertising board has been turned inside-out: a big roof with a beam and parapet height of 2.0 metres is the dominant design element. Sponsors can advertise and demonstrate their support of junior teams on the popular Laaerbergstraße.

The roof cantilevers out a few metres on all sides, and forms a generous, weather-resistant perimeter for entrances and terraces. On the eastern wing, a compact roof construction over the storage spaces is utilised as a roof terrace, where coaches and visitors are afforded a clear view over the heated artificial pitch.

The training hall forms the heart of the building and enjoys glare-free north light. The other sides are extremely compact and efficiently arranged - a cafeteria, offices, fitness rooms and massage and storage rooms. The access corridor on the ground floor works like a gallery to the sunken playing field. The required emergency escape for the offices and fitness rooms is organised in a series terraces. The sports hall with its artificial grass floor and birch plywood-impact protection walls provides the ideal atmosphere and a platform for concentrated training without distraction.

Low-temperature wall heating is utilised rather than conventional air heating. The artificial turf is carried through to the circulation zone, which operates as a pre-warming buffer zone. All changing areas have natural daylight and direct access to the outside even though they are located in the basement. This is made possible because of the wide ramp that doubles up as a means of delivery and an ideal sprint training zone.

Rainwater from the 2,500-suqare-metre roof surface is collected in large 120,000-liter tanks and serves as irrigation for the grass. The entire building is served by district heating.

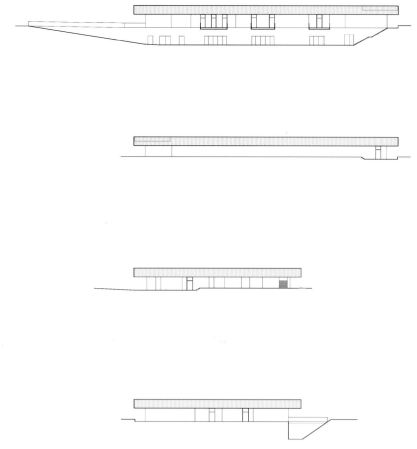

1. Exterior football field
2. Exterior view of the building
3. The building is small but solid

2

3

1. Foyer
2. Canteen
3. Gallery
4. Vold soccer hall
5. Office
6. Sauna, relaxation room
7. Massage
8. Fitness
9. Storage

1. Many "bridges" suspended from the building
2. Interior football field
3. Sunlight shining from outside

Slowtecture M

Designer: Shuhei Endo Architect Institute **Location:** Miki-city, Hyogo, Japan **Completion:** 2007
Photographer: Shuhei Endo Architect Institute **Site area:** 1,124,000 m² **Building area:** 16,168m²

This complex is to serve as an emergency staging area in case of future disaster. Relief operations require a vast space enables assumed/un-assumed activities in case of emergency. In Hyogo Prefecture, it has been prepared for various disasters from the experience of the Great Hanshin-Awaji Earthquake. The site is improved as "Miki Disaster Management Park Beans Dome" which is for a stronghold of emergent operation. It was a perquisite condition to combine a function of sports activities with original function from the beginning of this project so that this complex is combined with tennis courts for regular use to utilise this vast space.

This complex was required to look through the space of nine tennis courts including a centre court of 1,500 seats. Generally, when a building with many seats is constructed, several legal restrictions are imposed. Many difficulties have been occurs on the process of creating the entire space without any barrier. In the middle of the dome, the centre court has been sunken 6 metres below ground level to clear this restriction. A standard space frame system covers the required space to obtain this vast space. Although this dome is used as tennis courts usually, in case of emergency, lorries are running in the dome and tents are pitched for relief and rescue corps.

The continuous surface of roof and wall is covered with plants on artificial soil in which the bark of Japanese cedar and cypress are mixed. Mixed soil with plant seeds of 10 kinds is sprayed on the slant of 70° in maximum. At the beginning of the spraying, the state of the surface was just black soil. After a half year, the plants becomes growing. This plant glasses of surface offers a necessary result of insulation at the area of user's activities. The plants cover the building up to the height of 20 metres on the south side. On the north side in which the direct ray is small, it covers up to the height of 4 metres. The result of insulation by this plant glasses is effective, so that the temperature of inside of the dome is approximately 30 centigrade, when the temperature of outside is 40 centigrade during high summer. Normally large interior space requires artificial lighting even during day time. Here, it obtains the required illumination by providing three large top lights to reduce the energy consumption of artificial lighting. Shading seal was pasted on the glass to reduce the temperature increased by direct rays of sun, in addition to this, louver openings are installed for gravitational ventilation around the top lights.

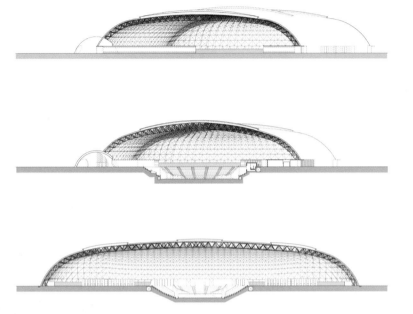

1. Bird view of the building
2. The building has grass wall
3. Roof of the building shining with sunlight

3

1. The yellow entrance
2. Yellow entrance structure details
3. Interior corridor

3

1. Entrance
2. Information
3. Office
4. Meeting room 1
5. Cafe
6. First-aid Station
7. Men's locker room
8. Women's locker room
9. Audio-visual room
10. Waiting room for lecturer
11. Meeting room 2
12. Nursing room
13. Studio

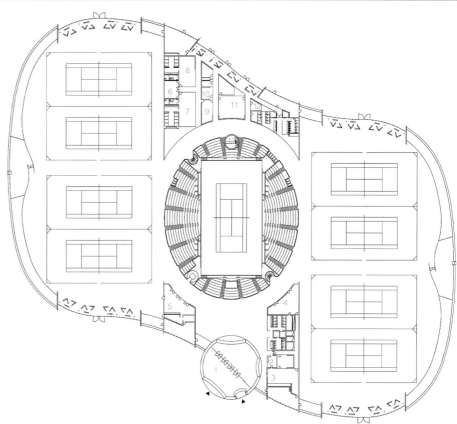

1,3. Tennis court
2. Interior part of the yellow entrance structure

3

Queensland Tennis Centre

Designer: Populous **Location:** Brisbane, Australia **Completion:** 2009 **Photographer:** Scott Burrows **Site area:** 37,084 m² **Building area:** 9,827m²

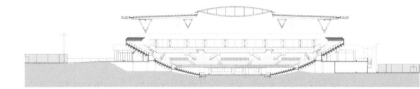

Tennis in Queensland has a new home, the purpose-built Queensland Tennis Centre, on Brisbane's Southside. Populous designed the international standard facility to ensure that it was benchmarked against the best in the world. The roof over the main arena, which acts as both a parasol and an umbrella, is the special feature of Centre Court, providing both the outdoor atmosphere of tennis and permanent shade cover. This Tennis Centres hosted the Brisbane International, a major tournament associated with the Australian Open Grand Slam.

The centre, on the site of the decommissioned Tennyson Power Station, is linked to a new luxury residential and parklands riverfront development. It is also the vehicle to provide a "nursery" for Queensland's future world champions, as well as international events. The facility is owned by the Queensland Government and managed by Stadiums Queensland.

The Populous team was led by Senior Principal, Andrew James, who says the inclusion of the "open roof" is both a cost effective and practical solution. "The fixed roof is partially solid (tin roof) and partially fabric (PTFE fabric). Insulation within the metal roof panels of the solid roof keeps the arena cooler and drier in summer, and cuts down the noise from the outside, particularly the heavy rain while retaining the intensity and theatre of the action inside. The fact the umbrella is "open" has also allowed us to make the best possible use of natural light," said Mr James. "The multipurpose nature of the tennis centre is another of its features, ensuring the facility is environmentally sustainable in the true sense of the word, because it can be used all year round by its community", he added.

The entire precinct has been designed with equitable accessibility in mind, both for spectators and players, with wheelchair tennis a growing professional sport. Wheelchair users and companions can access their seats directly off street level, without the use of lifts.

The tennis centre features all three "Grand Slam" surfaces – grass, clay and cushioned acrylic hard court. There are a total of twenty-two matches and training courts, most of which can be used daily by the local community, as well as dressed up for major events. The masterplan also allows for additional uses of the facility in the future.

Awarded:

2009 Queensland Steel Awards – Structural Design Award
2009 Queensland Engineering Excellence Awards – Building and Structures

1. View of Pat Rafter Arena across Training Academy
2. Pat Rafter Arena Spectator Precinct
3. Front Elevation Pat Rafter Arena

1. Terrace
2. Function
3. Meeting
4. Suite
5. Plant
6. Future wet bar
7. Kitchen pantry
8. Bar
9. PWD
10. Access to roof

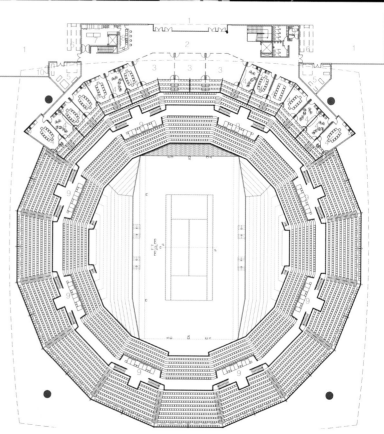

1. View of Centre Court Pat Rafter Arena
2. Interactive Museum
3. Corporate Suite

New Sports Hall

Designer: AGM architects **Location:** Zrenjanin, Serbia **Completion:** 2009 **Photographer:** Vladimir Popovic, Vladimir Vukoje **Building area:** 7,281.67m²

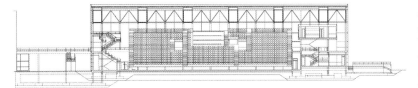

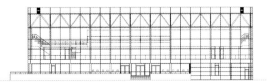

The design of the New Sports Hall reflects tradition of antique public forum that, besides sports events, includes various public contents, upgrading the offer of Zrenjanin city. In the same time, that kind of diversity and variety within the new complex, increasing the level of urbanity, makes possible to be less dependent on the weak city budget, which is very important for its sustainability.

Placed near the old hall of sports, with the City Stadium behind, the new hall establishes spatial order in the Park Zone, making the exploitation of the area more urban and sophisticated. Although the spatial structure of the hall is rather conventional, with centripetal scheme of sports field in the middle and auxiliary space around it, unexpectedly, the inner spatial elements, within their own envelopes of various characteristics, are acting as "houses within a house" The New Hall of Sports is designed as reduced, primary geometric shape, with outer membrane serving as a reference system for its dynamic internal anatomy. Transparency reduces the impression of the volume size, reflecting the surrounding landscape and making inner space visible from the outside, at the same time.

Structural concept is oriented towards the optimal relation between simple and efficient process of building, as well as the minimum share of imported components and hi-skilled works. Construction system is combined. Based on the single foundations system, couples of reinforced concrete pillars are supporting the spatial frames of roof carriers.

The Hall is opened in the summer of 2009, with basketball matches of the 25th Universiade in Belgrade and other Serbian cities.

Awarded:
2009 Ranko Radovic Award
2010 Award of 32. Salon of Architecture, Belgrade.
2010 First Place on the List of "Top Ten" of the Year in Architecture, NIN January 2010
2010 Award of Company Novosti - Best Realised Architectural Work in 2009

1. Transparent wall of the building
2. Main entrance ramp
3. Day view from the street

1

2

1. Day view from south
2. Entrance hall view from above

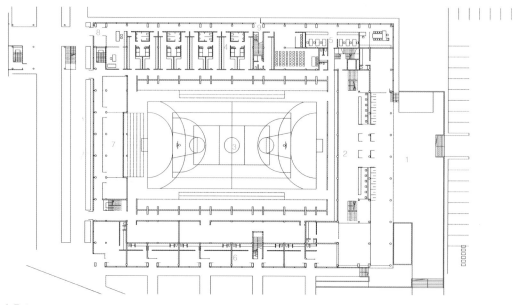

1. Entrance - open space
2. Entrance hall
3. Court
4. Locker room
5. Offices
6. Shops
7. Equipment
8. Athletes entrance
9. VIP entrance

2

1. Upper level of the entrance hall
2. Basketball court
3. Grand stands surround the court
4. Stands

EMÜ Sports Hall

Designer: Salto AB/ Maarja Kask, Karli Luik, Ralf Lõoke **Location:** Tartu, Estonia **Completion:** 2009
Photographer: Kaido Haagen, Reio Avaste & Karli Luik **Site area:** 27,000 m² **Building area:** 4600 m²

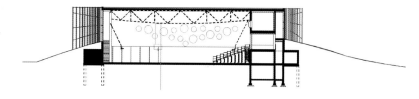

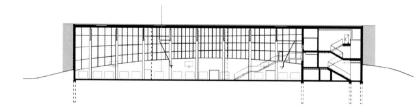

The buildings of the Estonian University of Life Sciences are located at the north-western edge of Tartu, bordering with Tähtvere Forest Park. The institution set out to integrate its campus and freshen its image with innovative architecture achieved with the help of open architectural competitions. In 2007, the competition for a new sports hall was held, followed by a competition for new auditorium annexes for the forestry building in 2008.

The chosen plot for the sports hall was an empty, flat field right at the roadside, the entrance to town, so in addition to functionality and ability to integrate and organise the surrounding campus area, the competition, in a way, expected a greater degree of representation than the building type would normally imply. At the same time, the spatial programme of a sports hall largely prescribes the possibilities of designing the main volume. The designers decided to stretch all corners of the cubic volume, and to integrate the building organically with landscape. DD Elevated ground forms a cushion for the slightly entrenched building, thus optically minimising its volume, and continues in undulating forms, encompassing outdoor sports grounds and bicycle paths, towards a sloping valley further away. The streched-out corners of the building create concave lines both in plan and elevation, gently relating to landscape and softening the size of the building. At the same time the building retains sharpness, enabling constantly varying, expressive views from various angles. This is due to optical effects of the form, clear-cut lines and finishing materials – glass on the longer sides of the building and larch cladding with wooden snags (nicknamed "hair") on the shorter ones. The latter also add to the subtle play of overall optical effects, being shorter and denser in the middle, and longer and more were widely placed at the edges. The snags coloured red form the name of the building – EMÜ spordihoone.

In the interior, the same attitude continues – a limited repertoire of considered details and takes. Moving around, the overall feel is light and airy, easy to navigate. The streched-out plan creates unconventional interior spaces. The choice of colours and materials is strictly limited to smooth exposed concrete and painted carroty surfaces with details in matte and shiny black. Irregularly placed bubbly interior windows opening towards the ballgames hall add a touch of frisky lightness and are echoed in the round glazed openings in gallery floor. In a delicate way, one is reminded that a sports hall is a bodily space – e.g. the concave outline of the building creates galleries narrowing in the middle, and with glazed openings in the floor the resulting space sharpens one's bodily experience of space.

1. Building façade
2. Path leading to the building

1. Transparent front wall of the building
2. Surrounding landscape of the building
3. Unique arch structure

1. Stairs
2. Training hall

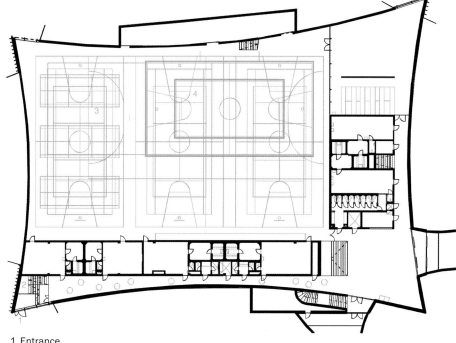

1. Entrance
2. Stair
3. Sports hall
4. Basketball hall

1. Small sports hall
2. Reception hall
3. Sports hall
4. Passage

Zamet Centre

Designer: 3LHD **Location:** Rijeka, Croatia **Completion:** 2009 **Photographer:** Damir Fabijanic, Domagoj Blazevic **Site area:** 12,289m² **Building area:** 16,830 m²

Situated in Rijeka's quarter Zamet, the new Zamet Centre in complete size of 16,830 square metres hosts various facilities: sports hall with max 2,380 seats, local community office, city library, 13 commercial and service facilities and a garage with 250 parking spaces.

One third of the sports hall's volume is cut in the ground, and other public facilities and services fully fit into the surrounding. The main architectural element of the Zamet Centre are "ribbons" stretching in a north-south direction, functioning at the same time as an architectural design element of the object and as a zoning element, which forms a public square and a link between the park on the north and school and B. Vidas Street on the south.

The ribbon-like stripes were inspired by "gromača", a type of rocks specific to Rijeka, which the centre was artificially reinterpreted by colour and shape. Stripes are covered with 51,000 ceramic tiles designed by 3LHD and manufactured specially for the centre. Steel girders of 55 metres span and different heights enable the natural light illumination of the sports hall.

The hall has been designed according to the latest world sports standards for major international sports competitions. The concept of the hall is based on flexibility of space. Space of the field is in size 46 metres x 44 metres, for two handball courts. The hall contains all the supporting facilities for professional training and competition, and auditorium designed as a system of telescopic stands enables the transformation for everyday use as well as for other activities such as concerts, conferences and congresses. Selected interior materials - wood and acoustic panels, suggest that the hall is a large living room for athletes. The main access to the hall and other facilities is located west of the hall from the public square and from the underground garage.

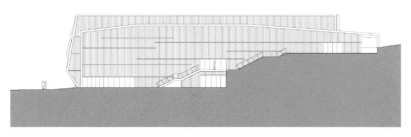

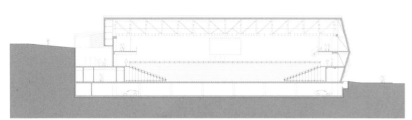

1. Bird view of the building
2. Exterior stairs
3. Entrance of the building

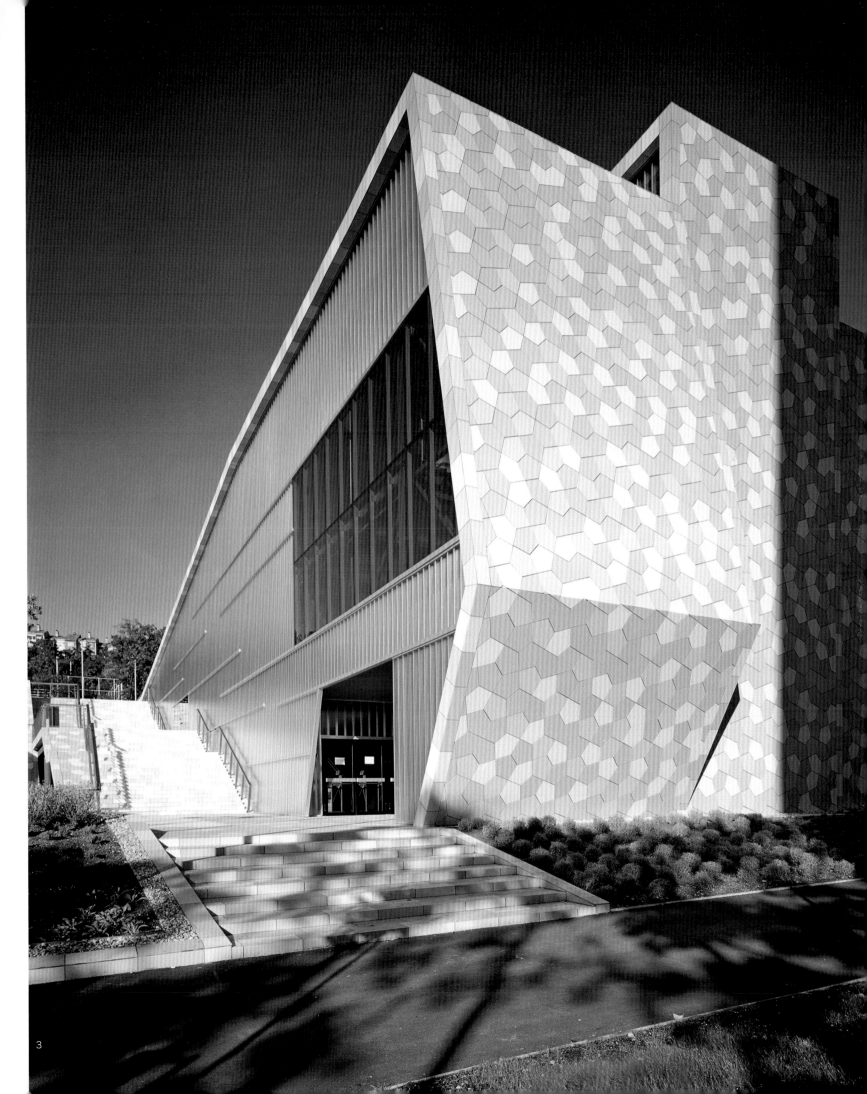

1. Bird view of the Zamet Centre
2. The building with surrounding landscape

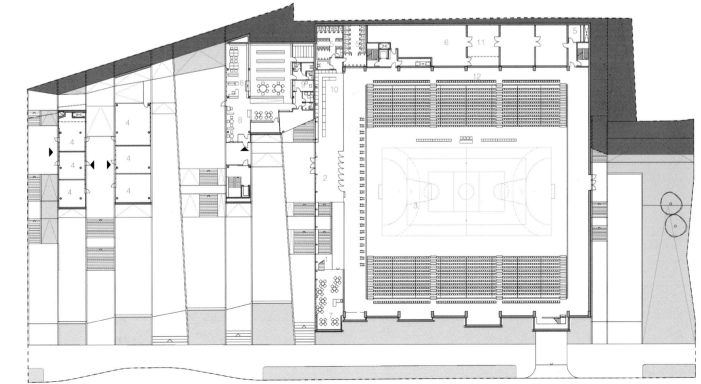

1. Staircase
2. Hall
3. Court
4. Retail
5. Toilet
6. Technical room
7. Refreshment place
8. Library
9. Office
10. Wardrobe
11. Technical courtyard
12. Spectators

1. Colorful sight at night
2. Exterior wall structure
3. Exterior staircase
4. Interior corridor

3

4

3

1. Seating close to the stairs
2. Passage
3. Relaxation seating

3

1. Playing court
2. Playing court with spectators seating
3. Side view of the court
4. People performing in the court

4

Podčetrtek Sports Hall

Designer: enota **Location:** Počdetrtek, Slovenia **Completion:** 2010 **Photographer:** Miran Kambič **Building area:** 3,570 m²

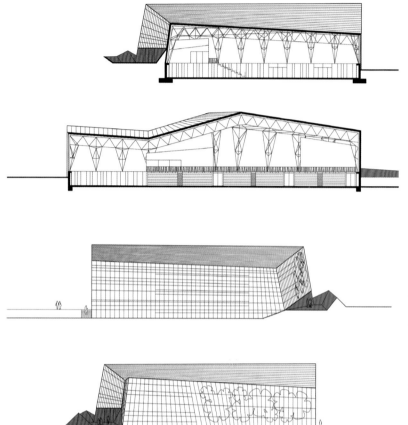

The municipal sports hall is located at the main road to Podčetrtek near Terme Olimia Spa Resort. It is located directly by the road, behind the existing roadside dyke. The main entrance itself is facing the road and is accessible via a connecting path between two driveways at the extreme points of the dyke.

Due to its size, which greatly exceeds the outlay of traditional constructions, it is impossible to look for similarities with indigenous surrounding architecture, but it seems logical to seek the design resemblances with larger facilities of the thermal complex. Especially the Termalija building, which is also located directly by the regional road. A specific dialogue is established between the two facilities. Termalija on one hand appears empty, light and colourful - almost playful, the municipal sports centre on the other hand acts rather serious - as a full, heavy, monolithic structure.

Its incidence is, to some extent, connected with the role and purpose it aspires to have in the city. Podčetrtek is a small town, and the new sports hall represents the single local indoor venue. Although primarily intended for sports activities, the main municipal hall will be also used for cultural events with larger number of visitors. It is this dual role that defines the platform for the specific design of the building. Its primary design element is a "red carpet", which leads visitors to the events in the building. The pathway that connects both driveways on the two extreme points is carved into the existing dyke. It is benefiting from the spatial anomaly and the dyke, thus shielding the entrance from the direct influence of the road. Spatially designed path, bounded by the dyke on one side, is incised in the building on the other side. Presented in vivid colours and attractive shapes it widens in front of the entrance to form a quality - almost square like area. An access platform that gradually embraces the visitors and directs them towards the main hall entrance.

The festivity of the access in the evenings is highlighted by a light ornament on the façade. Perforated cladding covering large window openings prevent the disturbing, direct impact of sun on the playgrounds throughout a day shines in distinctive flower patterns at dusk. The indoor developments are thus directly reflected on the façade and added to the promotion of events, as well as the attractiveness of the facility.

1. Building façade
2. Black wall contrasts with the vivid colour of the path
3. Narrow view of the faraway hill

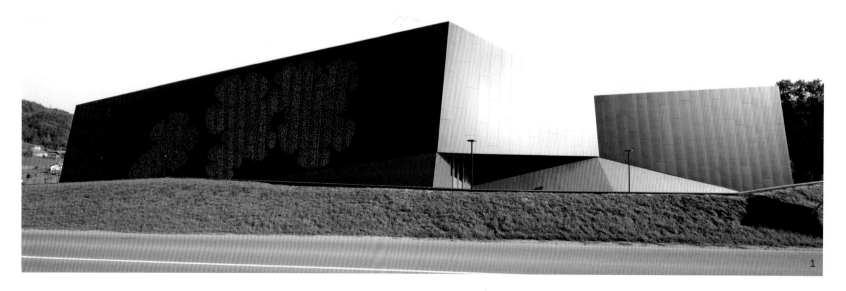

1

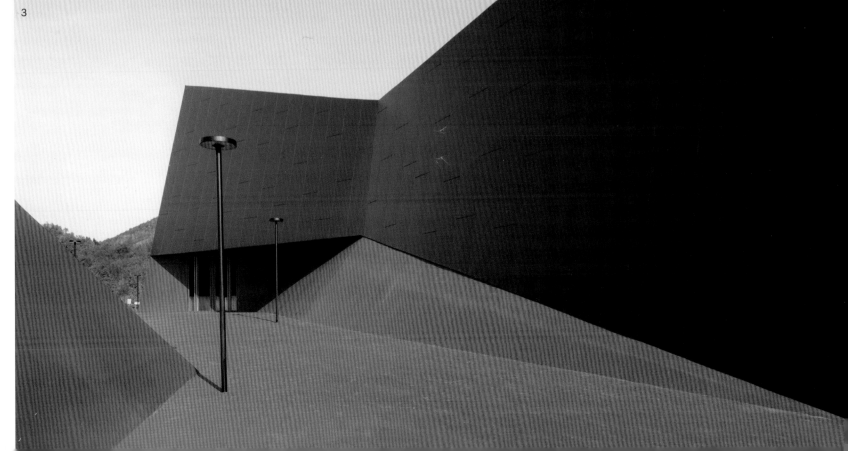

1 Perforated cladding at daylight
2. Perforated cladding at night
3. Perforated cladding looks bright at night

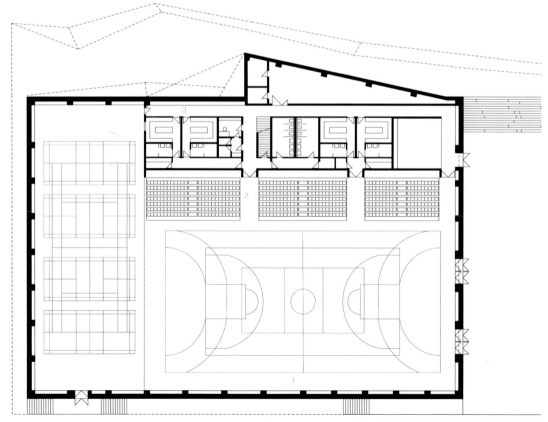

1. Playground
2. Spectators seats
3. Lounge

1

1 Sports hall
2. Stairs
3. Lower playing court seen from the upper level
4. Passage

1. The hall
2. The playing court

2

Orense Swimming Pools for Vigo University

Designer: Francisco José Mangado Beloqui **Location:** Orense, Spain **Completion:** 2008 **Photographer:** Pedro Pegenaute, Roland Halbe **Site area:** 2,800 m²

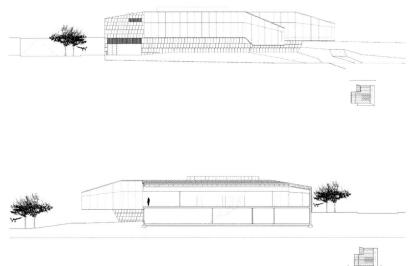

The plot chosen is at the highest point of the university campus, a location that gives it a special value in the relationship between the city of Orense and the campus, currently encumbered by the presence of a busy road between them. Opting for a programme oriented towards leisure, and that may thereby serve both the university community and the people of Orense will help to heighten the value of the building as an element of urban interaction.

This special location has inspired the main conceptual and formal decisions of the project. The proposal is drawn up as a vast platform that looks onto the campus, and the whole organisation of functions is indebted to this idea. The users will be able to see the campus and its buildings from this raised platform, which contain the swimming pools. The platform is designed with bold projections supported by a strong base that, aside from spanning the existing drops, shapes the pools and contains all the water treatment services and necessary systems for the correct performance of the programme. The contrast between this massive, topographic base and the cantilevering light glass surfaces surrounding the public level of swimming pools is one of the basic formal arguments of the project.

The access to the pool from the highest area allows accommodating the main functions in a single floor. The complementary uses – changing rooms and restrooms – follow an L-shape. Embraced by these are the poolside spaces, "floating" beyond the structural and functional limits imposed.

The roof is the central element. Seen from the top floors of the housing blocks fronting the plot it becomes the façade and main image of the building. From the interior, acting as ceiling of the pools, its geometry seeks a prominent role by defining a space that is detached and projected towards the campus.

Vast concrete at the base, glass and wood compose the material palette that were used both inside and outside.

Awarded:

2010 FAD Architecture Award

The FAD awards were created in 1958 with the aim of promoting the avant-garde tendencies of the time and to acknowledge high quality works in the new paths and investigations that were opening up and transforming the traditional forms and languages of design.

1. View into the interior from the transparent wall
2. Transparent glass wall
3. Overview of the building
4. Side view of the building

1

2

4

1. Recreational swimming pool
2. Competition swimming track
3. View of outside from the swimming pool

3

1. Vestibule
2. Circulation
3. Waiting zone
4. Infirmary
5. Dressing room
6. Swimming pool 16*9
7. Bathing zone
8. Swimming pool 25*16
9. Terrace

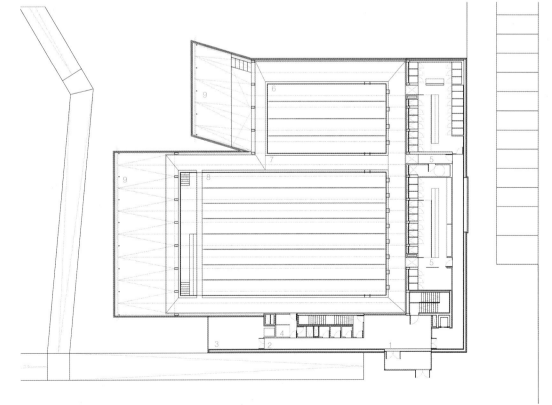

Municipal Pools of Povoação

Designer: barbosa & guimarães——josé antónio barbosa · pedro lopes guimarães **Location:** Povoação · Portugal **Completion:** 2008 **Photographer:** João Ferrand **Site area:** 385,700m²

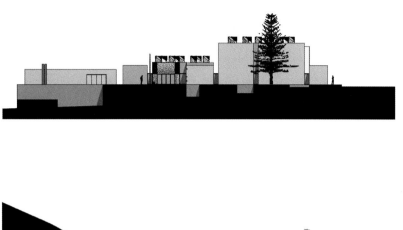

The village of Povoação is located on the Archipelago of the Azores, on the southern edge of the island of S. Miguel.

Protected from the sea by a slope, the building is going to occupy a plot comprised of a flat, rectangular platform already prepared and used by the Municipal Council for other outdoor sports activities. This platform was achieved by "sacrificing" the slope, imposing a cut that distorts its natural volume.

The project takes advantage of the existing cut to construct the building along its length, seeking a "fusion" between the new construction and the surrounding landscape.

Its volume is fragmented and "runs", forming masses of black basalt, which correspond to the various functional groups of the programme.

The coverings are "contaminated" by the green of the surrounding fields, punctuated by skylights, which ensure natural lighting of the interior spaces.

A square of basalt gives physical support to the building, defining courses and accesses around an Araucaria, whose verticality and symbolic load announce and upgrade this new public space.

Inside, the programme is organised from the competition and training tanks, maintaining basalt as the dominant element in the entire composition.

On the upper floor, an outdoor esplanade supporting the bar looks out to sea.

The first challenge was to solve the planning issues, especially, to create an appropriate entrance. The original opening to the leased space was at the corner of the building, quite distant from the building's striking stone-arched main entrance. The designers won Historical Board's approval to close the secondary doorway and modify the primary entrance and lobby area. Inside the traditional Victorian oak doors, the designers created a new divided vestibule with a security to the office building and a stunning new passageway leading to Rain itself. To the right, a glossy pebble-finished wall rises above a steel trough of river rocks and bears simple acrylic cut-outs of the restaurant's logo elements.

1. Bird view of the building
2. Grass roof of the building

2

1. Little plaza outside the building
2. Children playing on the roof
3. The building with surrounding landscape

3

1. Swimming
2. Entrance
3. Dinning
4. Reception

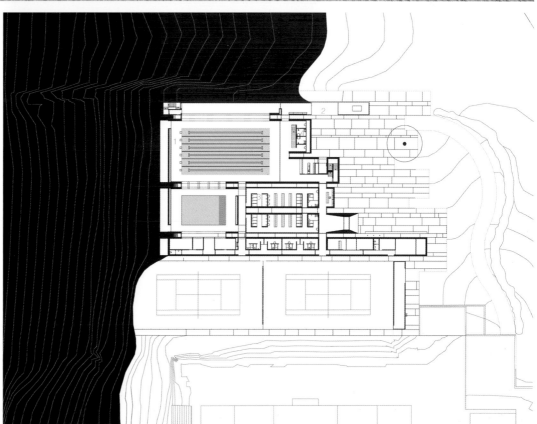

1

1. Entrance
2. Passage
3. Swimming pool with rest seats
4. Shower

1. Swimming track
2. Recreational pool
3. Clear water in the recreational pool

Expansion of Centre Sportif J.C. Malépart

Designer: Saïa Barbarese Topouzanov Architectes **Location:** Quebec, Canada **Completion:** 2010
Photographer: Frederic Saia, Marc Cramer, Vladimir Topouzanov **Site area:** 2,680 m²

Architectural firm Saia Barbarese Topouzanov was asked to work on the expansion of the Centre Sportif Jean-Claude Malépart, named for the member of the National Assembly who defended the rights of the disadvantaged in his Sainte-Marie riding.

The 1996's building was to become a sort of crossroads that would continue to serve the existing facilities – gym and community halls – while giving access to a new ticket booth, a half-Olympic-size swimming pool, and a wading pool, along with a changing rooms, training room, a room for lifeguards, a storage area, and spaces for related services.

The new building had to complement the surrounding urban fabric and form a unit with the articulated volumes of the 1996 sports centre. The main entrance on Rue Ontario, without changing location, gained visibility. In fact, the transparent wall where it was currently extended the length of the new façade and stretched, with its height diminishing to Rue du Havre. The resulting sharp corner oriented the eye toward the entrance, which was thus enhanced.

The expansion forms a simple, diaphanous volume. It allows clear identification of the entities created and the dialogue between them. On the outside, it adopts the scale of neighbouring structures. It reaches its maximum elevation along Rue Ontario. From there, a variable geometry gently inclines the roof to make it compatible with the two- and three-storey structures on Rue du Havre; to refer to the curved roof of the gym; and to provide the gym block with natural light and the adjacent garden with maximum sunlight. This linear, functional garden has become a structuring axis for the various components of the site. The opaque upper part of the skin is in a pale tone that helps to reduce heat loss into the environment.

The idea of waves, inspired by a David Hockney painting, Portrait of an artist: both indoors and outdoors, a wave develops on the perimeter of the building, rising and falling in two continuous undulations.

The dialogue between the new building and the old one, between the continuous movement impressed upon the recent volume and the more jagged, broken-up movement of the old one, continues in the properties of the materials selected. The grey-tinted glass harmonises with the colours of the earlier structure. It gives passers-by an idea of what is going on inside while preserving some privacy for users. The milky tone and reflective quality of the upper wall are echoed in the material for the roof to ensure the extension from one to the other in contrast with the clear demarcations of the building erected fourteen years ago.

This architectural project is, above all, people-oriented. The project is even more concerned with the wellbeing and health of users. The construction process, the systems implemented, and the air and water recycling were all designed with sustainable development in mind.

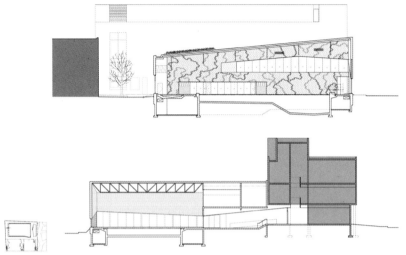

1. The building is located along the street
2. Pattern of the exterior wall
3. Façade

1

1. Retail
2. Passage
3. Corridor of the bathroom
4. Male bathroom entrance

2

3

4

1. Swimming pool
2. The interior wall extends the pattern of exterior wall
3. Light shining above the water
4. From the swimming pool people could see outside via the window

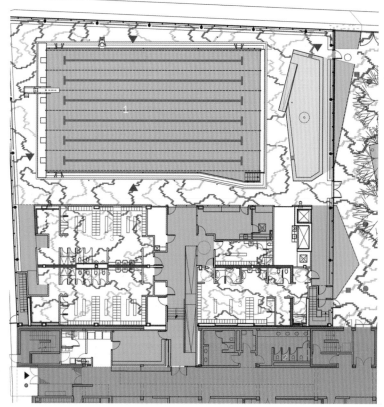

1. Swimming pool
2. Toilet
3. Dressing room
4. Entrance

1. Birdview of the swimming pool
2. Jump stand
3. Leisure pool beside the swimming pool

3

Torre Pellice Ice Palace

Designer: Claudio Lucchin & architetti associati **Location:** Torre Pellice, Italy **Completion:** 2006
Photographer: Paolo Quartana **Building area:** 16,776 m²

The ice rink is designed as a structure for community service and sports. The building was used as a hockey arena during the Olympic Games, and afterwards it continued to be used professionally by local teams. The main formal reference for the building is the environment, which is understood as the sum of the formal, historical and cultural values of the site: the profile of the surrounding mountains, the colour of the stones, the greenery and the plant species all define a new shape that is articulated in the large blocks that resemble stones embedded together almost like a rocky outcropping rising out of the earth. The three block-shaped structures are aligned on three different axes that are inherent in the existing constructed area: the "croix de ville", the main road towards the mountaintop where the Waldenses community has built its symbols and the confines of the lot itself. The central position of the building on the lot creates two large plazas. From the interior, the plazas look like the natural extension of the playing field. The roots of the site are represented not only in the materials, they are also furthered in the relationship with the external light assuring the use of the structure for training as well.

Awarded:
IPC/IAKS Special Distinctions 2007
The IAKS is awarding the IPC/IAKS Distinction for sports facilities suitable for persons with a disability. The IPC/IAKS Distinction aims to promote accessibility to sports facilities and all other buildings in order to give people with a disability the opportunity to practise or view sport without limitation or barriers.

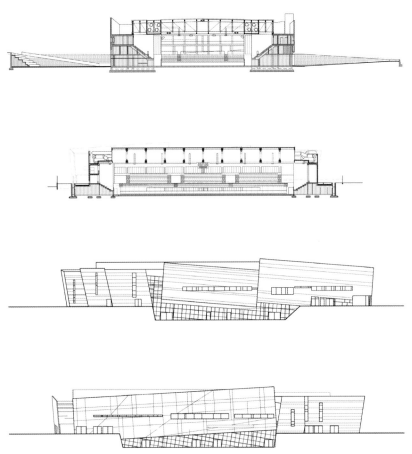

1. North entrance
2. East side
3. West side

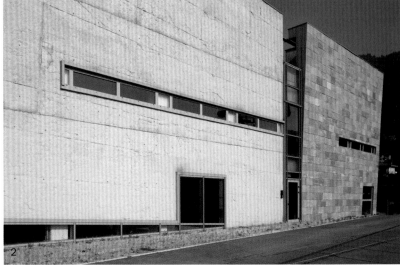

1. South side
2. South façade
3. North façade with surrounding landscape

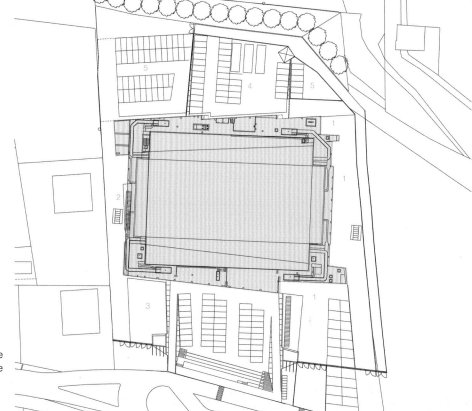

1. Home team supporters entrance
2. Guest team supporters entrance
3. Restaurant
4. Bus parking area
5. Athlete parking area

1

1 South entrance
2 Interior hall
3. Playing court

2

Majori Primary School Sports Ground

Designer: SIA Substance **Location:** Jurmala, Latvia **Completion:** 2008 **Photographer:** SIA Substance; Maris Lapins; Martins Kudrjavcevs **Site area:** 3,252 m²

Jurmala is a popular Latvian sea resort on the coast of Baltic sea. It is located on a narrow slip of land between the sea and the river, and each year attracts thousands of tourists from both Latvia and neighbouring countries. Jurmala City Council contracted the designers to build a sports ground that may be used all year long in any weather. Therefore, they constructed the sports ground with a shed that opens to the river, and is closed towards the nearby railway. In warm season the sports ground floor has a syntetic covering suitable for athletics, basketball, volleyball and handball, but in cold season it is turned into artificial ice ground for hockey and ice-skating. The sports ground is located on a square opposite Majori primary school – an abandoned market place. One of the historic market buildings had to be preserved to perpetuate the fact that this place was used to be a market place. Therefore, the designers adapted one of the buildings to accommodate changing rooms for teams and coaches, sports inventory storage and rent, and public vestibil with administrator's workplace. The second floor of the building accomodates spectators stands.

Although the structure of the object is concise, it has several conceptual layers that include symbolic, landscape, functional and architectonic aspects. The object has a strategically significant location because it is visible from all passing to Jurmala: the railway, the city's main street and the river that has live boat traffic with the capital of Latvia Riga. The object is a significant accent in the city's overall landscape, and consequently its shape and siluet are especially important. For that reason, the designers looked for symbols typical for Jurmala and found amber – chrystalised resin of pine. Pine-trees up to 30 metres tall are typical for Jurmala and for most of Latvian sea coast, and amber may often be found washed ashore the sea coast.

The total building site of the sports ground is 3,252 square metres. It is a rather prominent volume compared to the surrounding 1-2 storey buildings. Therefore, it was important to integrate the object into the existing landscape by reducing its height. The variable height of the shed is a peculiar compromise between the heights necessary for sports games and the surrounding low-storey buildings.

As the object is large, it was important to create it light. It is characteristic to broad-span roof structures to have a mess of constructions and communications at the ceiling. The designers thought that it would look dramatic in a building with varying height and decided to leave the constructive frames outside and to lag the shed from inside. It resulted in a clear and dynamic interior, while the external open-work frames significantly reduced bulkiness of the building. The polycarbonate used in the building has a 60% transparency. At night it becomes an original screen of light accenting its shape in the city's landscape.

Awarded:
Short-listed for Latvia's Best Architecture 2007 Prize in Category "New Buildings"
Nominated for the Final of International Architecture Prize "Arhpremia 2008" (RUS) in Category "Innovation of Public Buildings"
Shortlisted for Mies van der Rohe Award 2009

1. The silhouette of this building resembles the huge amber
2. The structure is not just a routine sporting venue, but a true local landmark
3. Building at night

1

2

3

1 A view from the Riga Street
2. Outside parking
3. View from the railway

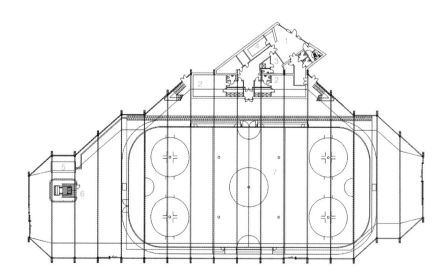

1 Foyer of main entrance
2. Wardrobe for athletes
3. Wardrobe for trainers
4. Stockroom and technical room
5. Compressor
6. Garage for the ice combine
7. Ice rink

1

2

1. The ice rink is useful for the local ice hockey teams too
2. Players are resting
3. Playing on the ice rink
4. The shed is open to the south and from the spectators stands you can see not only the rink but the nearest landscape too

3

4

Multifonctional Complex La Maladiere

Designer: Geninasca Delefortrie SA **Location:** Neuchatel, Switzerland **Completion:** 2007 **Photographer:** Thomas Jantscher **Building area:** 105,000m²

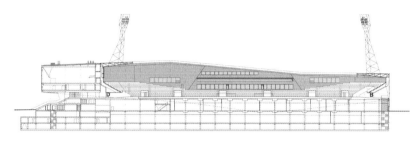

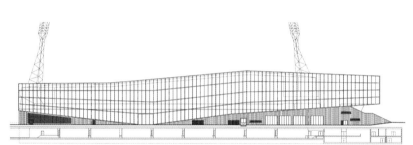

On the ground floor, the main proposal is a glistening skin made of glass and aluminium reflecting the city, where as the superior façades in diaphanous reveals the presence of the stadium in the back ground: this evocative skin makes up the casket for "the instrument of the sportive show".

By its position, its configuration and its expression, the project was organised to precisely match all these different characteristics. The project defines in the west, a street space, meeting the proportions of the existing streets. It suggests in the east, an esplanade to handle the flow between the new complex and the port area. In the north and south, it follows the lines and the geometry of the existing axes. The presence of this building, important by its size and function, enables the designers to reorganse a place, which has now vanished and to give a new meaning to the town's entry.

The base of the complex incorporates the mall, the rescue services and fire station, the delivery platforms and the 930-place car park. The first floor is dedicated to the football pitch, the access to the galleries (12,000 seats), the bars and the restrooms. The second floor incorporates the administrative offices and changing rooms for the sports facilities.

The third and fourth floors include the six gymnastic halls and the VIP activities. In order to find the correct scales and to represent the different functions of the building, the architectural expression suggests a building, which plays with reflection and the transparency.

The base allows the mirrored skin made of glass and stainless steel to reflect the town.

The upper façade's skin is made from translucent woven metal wire revealing the stadium, enabling it to be seen from another side. The stadium is treated as if it is an Italian theatre and coloured in red and black, which allows the spectator to become immersed in the world of entertainment.

Awarded:
Charles Duyer Award 2008
IAKS AWARD Bronze Medal 2009

1. Bird view
2. Entrance

1

1 The building is located along the street
2. View of the exterior wall
3. Building façade

2

1. Football field
2. Spectators seating
3. Entrance
4. WC

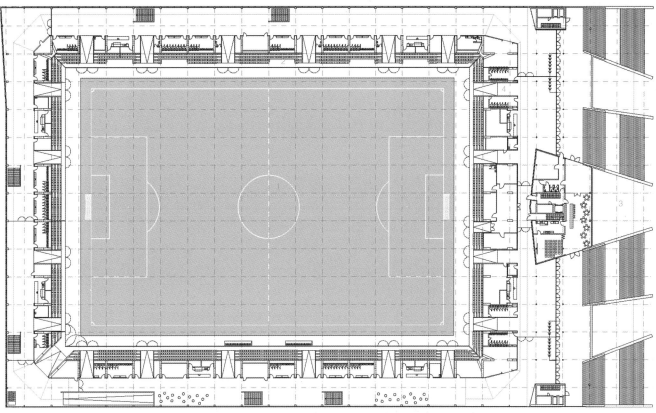

1. The football field
2. The football field with grand auditorium
3. Passage hall

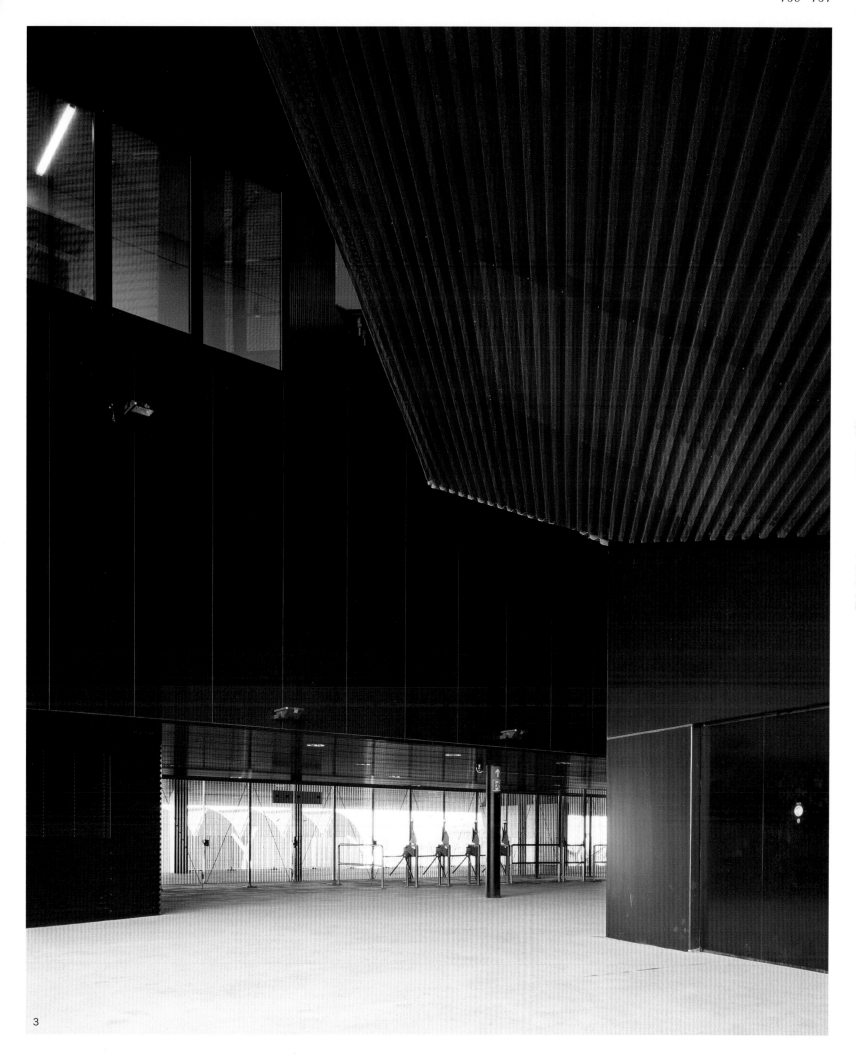

3

1. Auditorium
2. Seats of the auditorium

Aberdeen Sports Village

Designer: Reiach and Hall Architects **Location:** Aberdeen, UK **Completion:** 2009 **Photographer:** Ioana Marinescu, Reiach and Hall **Site area:** 2.1 ha **Building area:** 17,650 m²

Aberdeen Regional Sports Facility is an award-winning major sports building of local and national importance. The facility has set a template for all such ventures in Scotland, and was selected as a training base for the 2012 Olympics. Civic, identifiable and welcoming, this is an uplifting sight in one of Aberdeen's deprived areas. The building's purpose, with its implications for health and wellbeing, is one that contributes to the cultural sustainability of the wider community, too.

At 210 metres long by up to 110 metres wide, this is a big building and the relatively short front marks the start of a route – an internal "street" that stretches the length of the building with the major rooms placed on either side. These rooms include a nine-court games hall, an indoor athletics facility (which includes a 135-metre long straight track) and a full size indoor football pitch with "3G" turf, along with the squash courts, a commercial fitness suite, offices and changing rooms that one would expect. There is a considerable degree of transparency between these various spaces so that the overall building is perceived as one whole rather than a series of parts.

Reiach and Hall's concern for context is often given an abstract presentation. Here, where the east elevation is 210 metres long and highly visible from along the coast, they sought a "dramatic, but quiet" presence. Using a photograph of the sky above the site, they isolated a strip in a computer programme, extruded it into bands of colour and then worked with Rodeca at their German factory, to match the colouring by adding minute proportions of pigment. The resultant ethereal blues, greys and whites work well in making subtle variations for the repetitive façade – and not only outside, but inside too, where the pale colours are revealed on the monochromatic and repeating structure.

Awarded:

Aberdeen Civic Society First Prize 2009
Roses Design Awards Best Health / Leisure Project 2010 Silver
Scottish Design Awards Best Public Building 2010 Commendation
RIBA Award 2010
RICS Award for Community Benefit – Highly Commended

1. The spectator stand and subtly coloured, translucent cladding panels
2. The "head" of the building is scaled to relate to the domestics houses in the rest of the street
3. The chequer pattern on the grey steel cladding helps to dematerialise the bulk of the building in the granite context of Aberdeen

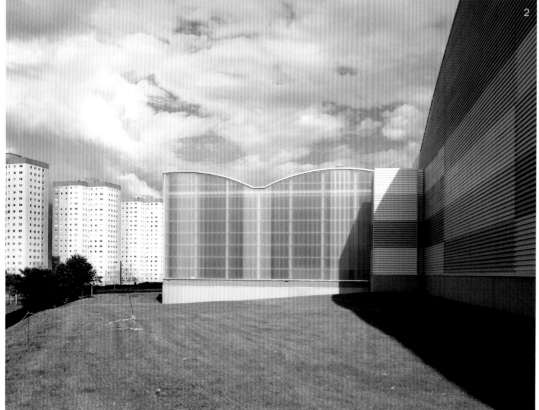

1. The colours of the cladding panels are sampled from a typical photograph of the sky above the site.
2. The building integrates with the sky
3. Exterior wall pattern
4. The entrance

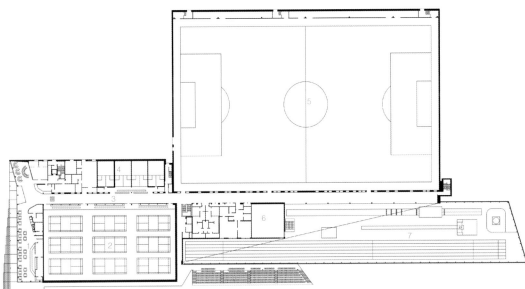

1. Cafe
2. Games hall
3. The 'street'
4. Squash
5. Football hall
6. Dojo
7. Athletics hall
8. 500-seat stand

1. Seats of the spectator stand
2. Multi-functional court
3. Café

3

1. Indoor football training field
2. Perforated wall of the football hall
3. Tracks
4. Indoor arena

Designer: Nadel Architects **Construction Drawings Design:** BIAD **Location:** Futian, Shenzhen, China
Completion: 2008 **Photographer:** Nadel Architects **Images:** Chaoying Yang **Building Area:** 69,062 m²
Arena: 5,000 Seats **Gymnasium:** 3,000 Seats **Swimming Pool:** 500 Seats **Hotel:** 300 Guestrooms

Futian Sports & Entertainment Complex

Designed by Nadel Architects, Futian Sports & Entertainment Complex is a new, 69,062-square-metre mixed use sports centre in the city of Shenzhen, just north of Hong Kong, China. The complex will be a world-class venue that attracts local and international athletes, sports spectators, shoppers and travellers alike. When it is fully completed, Futian will offer not only a full range of athletic facilities, but also include entertainment, retail and hospitality venues.

Sponsored by the City of Shenzhen, the massive complex will be completed in multiple phases. The first phase, completed in March 2008, consists of a 3,000-seat basketball and tennis arena, concert hall with seating for 2,500 pectators, a natatorium with an Olympic size swimming pool and seating for 500 spectators, rooftop tennis courts with dedicated locker rooms and parking, bowling alley, archery range, badminton courts, an outdoor soccer field with a 5,000-seat stadium and a 1,280-square-metre health club with fitness training, spa, and saunas. From the exposed steel structure and robust use of concrete and glass to the sleek, curvo-linear shape, Futian Sports & Entertainment Complex has already helped to redefine the urban fabric of Shenzhen by appealing to the city's edgier, more youthful crowds.

Nadel's core vision for Futian was to provide a connection between two active, dense neighbourhoods, while providing visual drama for the triangular site by utilising a unique set of shapes and forms. The resulting z-shaped plan restores the urban fabric with juxtaposed rigid and curvy forms that emphasize connections between the neighbourhoods and various venues. Thus, the dynamic interplay of the architectural shapes provides the backdrop for an iconic entertainment and cultural centre for its citizens and tourists.

Since Futian caters to young, athletic people, the design needed to reflect this in its vibrancy. The space-age appearance, with its silver tones and shimmering glass, clearly makes a visual impact. But the robust forms also encourage exploration and serve as a reminder that this is a highly accessible community space.

Although sustainability wasn't one of the main goals, the design did benefit from green features. The rooftop park space serves as insulation, regulating temperatures below. The venues take advantage of natural light, and operable windows let air flow through the buildings. Nadel's work on the project has already been recognised by the Society of American Registered Architects for design excellence.

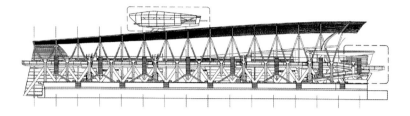

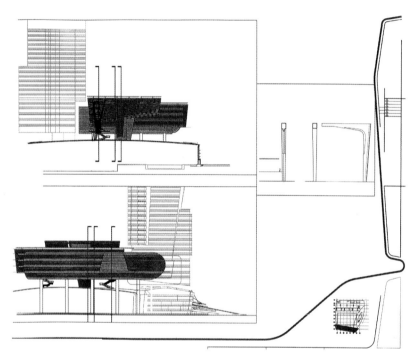

1. Administration building
2. Natatorium hall
3. Entrance to offices

3

1. View from sports field (left)
2. View from sports field (right)
3. Stairs to rooftop plaza

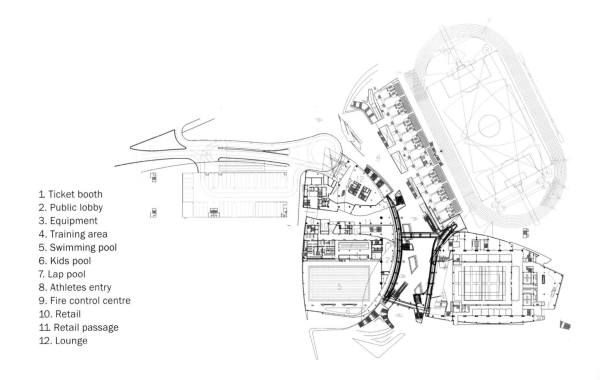

1. Ticket booth
2. Public lobby
3. Equipment
4. Training area
5. Swimming pool
6. Kids pool
7. Lap pool
8. Athletes entry
9. Fire control centre
10. Retail
11. Retail passage
12. Lounge

Berry Sports and Recreation Hall

Designer: Allen Jack + Cottier Architects **Location:** NSW, Australia **Completion:** 2008 **Photographer:** Nic Bailey **Site area:** 60 hectares

Berry Sports and Recreation Hall, designed by Allen Jack+Cottier (AJ+C), has won the 2009 World Architecture Festival Award for Best Sports Building.

Set on 60 hectares of rolling countryside in Berry, three hours south of Sydney in Australia, the site was originally an experimental dairy farm and has made way for a magical and innovative multipurpose hall for basketball, netball, rock climbing, dance and theatre.

Reminiscent of a modern farm shed, the building comprises two long sides of precast concrete panels, each pierced by 500 shards of glass in amoeba-like windows, allowing natural light to flood the halls in the day and interior lights to shine through at night, illuminating the building and making it "disappear" into the night sky.

The structure reflects that year's festival theme "Less does more", and shows how innovative and cost effective design can transform the architectural landscape, marrying the realities of environmental and economic necessity.

Michael Heenan, project architect and a principal of AJ+C, said "This project shows how we can do more with less, using cost effective precast concrete to transform a building into an iconic structure, providing a template that can be used for future projects."

The building also features environmentally sustainable design (ESD), with a dozen wind turbines combining with panels of louvers to create a natural ventilation system, which cools the structure in summer and creates an insulation blanket in winter. Roof water is tracked back from the 3.5-metre cantilevered composite roof via a steel beam to provide water for irrigation tanks.

Awarded:

Australian Institute of Architects (NSW) Public Architecture Award, 2008
Blacket Award for Regional Architecture, 2008
World Architecture Festival Awards, 2009
World Architecture Festival is being launched as an annual event by Emap, the media group, which runs other festivals including the World Retail Congress and Cannes Lions International Advertising Festival. WAF is the most well-known festival in the world.

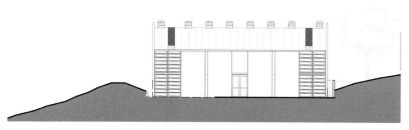

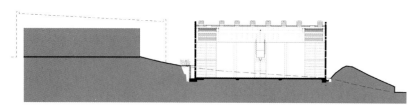

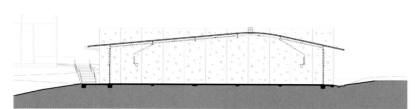

1. Outdoor playing filed
2. Perforated wall

1

3

1. Back of the building
2. Entrance
3. Path to the building

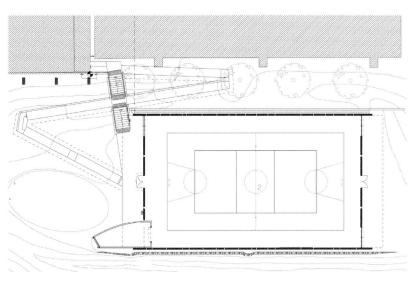

1. Entrance
2. Sports court
3. Staircase

1. Indoor climbing wall
2. Indoor playing court
3. Basketball court

University of Maine Student and Recreation Centre

Designer: Cannon Design **Location:** Orono, USA **Completion:** 2007 **Photographer:** Esto Photography Inc. /Anton Grassi **Building area:** 8,083m²

Cannon Design provided planning and design services for the largest building project ever undertaken at the University of Maine at Orono: a new 8,083-square-metre Student Recreation and Fitness Centre featuring a three-court gymnasium, a multipurpose athletic court, fitness centre, natatorium, walking/jogging track, two racquetball courts, and support spaces. The contemporary, LEED Silver certified building fits seamlessly into its heavily wooded site and incorporates sustainable building materials and systems, including heat-recovery systems and recyclable materials.

Extensive use of glass on the south façade presents views of the activities within and provides users with views out to the scenic campus. The building's exterior material palette of architectural precast concrete panels, copper metal cladded panels, field stone, and glass walls harmonise with the natural setting. Inside, exposed wood structure, wood paneling, and wood flooring evoke a natural, organic ambiance.

Two double-height, skylighted galleries - one north-south and one east-west - form the primary circulation. A main stair and elevator at the intersection of the two galleries provide access to the second level. A centrally located control desk provides views of the lobby and lounge areas, the main elevator and stair, and the entrances to the fitness area and three-court gymnasium. A free zone adjacent to the control desk offers access to the director's office, staff offices, a conference room, and a multipurpose room.

The weight-training room, which houses both free weights and circuit training machines, offers users views into the adjacent three-court gymnasium and outside to the surrounding campus and woods. The cardiovascular fitness area on the upper level, open to the weight-training area on the ground floor, affords views of the campus, the jogging track and gym, and the north-south gallery. A three-court gymnasium accommodates basketball and volleyball. Divider curtains allow courts to be used for a variety of other activities. A jogging track suspended above the three-court gymnasium gives joggers views through clerestory windows to the east and the forest to the north.

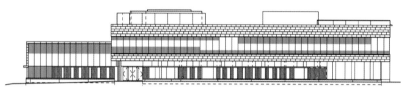

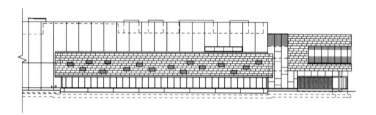

1. Side view of the building
2. Courtyard
3. Soft light shining on the wall
4. Solid exterior wall of the building

1

2

1. Basketball court
2. Stair up to the gym
3. Volleyball court

3

1. Entry vestibule
2. Lobby
3. Control desk
4. Juice bar/ vending
5. Conference
6. Offices
7. Stair
8. Elevator
9. Circulation
10. Men's restroom
11. Men's locker room/showers
12. Women's restroom
13. Women's locker room/showers
14. Leisure pool
15. Pool storage
16. Pool mechanical
17. Pool office
18. Assisted changing
19. Multipurpose room
20. Weight training
21. 3-court gym
22. Multipurpose activity court
23. First aid
24. Equipment check-out
25. Equipment
26. Mechanical
27. Gym storage

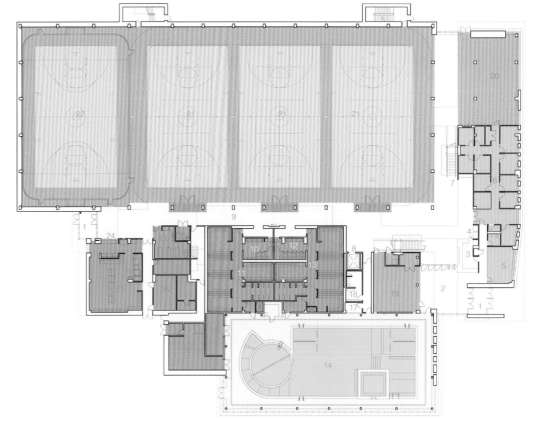

1 Swimming hall
2. Gym
3. Fitness facilities next to the window provide views of the outside

University of Wisconsin Oshkosh Student Recreation and Wellness Centre

Designer: Cannon Design **Location:** Oshkosh, WI, USA **Completion:** 2007 **Photographer:** James Steinkamp **Building area:** 9,383m²

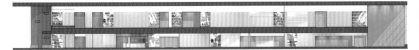

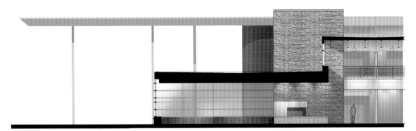

The new 9,383-square-metre Student Recreation and Wellness Centre at the University of Wisconsin, Oshkosh is focused on providing a pleasant, supportive, and convenient campus location for non-athlete students, staff, and faculty to exercise - in organised programmes or independently - in a vibrant social atmosphere.

Sited along the Fox River, which borders the campus on the west side, and within easy walking distance from the campus residence halls, the building provides the campus with a symbolic "front door" for approaching visitors crossing the river. Its clear visibility from numerous points on campus makes it a beacon in the evenings, when much of the campus's recreational activity occurs. The building's river location forges a strong point of connection with one of the campus most attractive natural amenities, offering panoramic river views for those involved in aerobic and cardiovascular exercise within.

Visitors entering at the first floor are immediately greeted by a public area, or free zone, offering a full view of all internal activities. A double-height cardio space beyond the main control point is situated to capitalise upon river views and is complemented by a climbing wall. A juice bar with a large stone fireplace beckons students to socialise and study before or after workouts. Other first-floor components include a 3-court gymnasium, a multipurpose athletic court, locker rooms, offices, and a weight theatre for heavy lifting. The second level provides access to multipurpose rooms and to a suspended running track that, in addition to offering users views of the campus and river, acts as an integrated, live exterior advertisement heralding the facility's identity as a destination for social interaction, wellness, and recreation.

The Centre's exterior makes reference to neighbouring campus architecture while maintaining a vibrant, modern appearance. Brick was painstakingly matched to that of other campus buildings. Limestone at the building's base was quarried from Fond du Lac, a mere 14 miles from campus. Copper panelling adorns the building's lakeside façade, while aluminum-and-glass curtainwall admits ample light to interior spaces and provides occupants with scenic views. Designed with numerous sustainable features, the building achieves the equivalent of a LEED Silver rating.

1. Night view of the building
2. Unique form of the building structure
3. Side view of the building

1

1. Gym and interior climbing rock wall
2. Rock climbing wall
3. Weight training hall

2

3

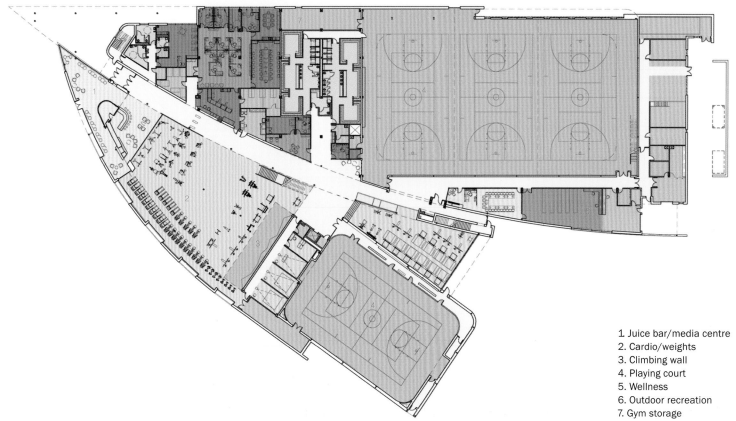

1. Juice bar/media centre
2. Cardio/weights
3. Climbing wall
4. Playing court
5. Wellness
6. Outdoor recreation
7. Gym storage

1. Gym
2. Volleyball hall
3. Juice bar
4. Running track

California State University, Long Beach, Student Recreation & Wellness Centre

Designer: Cannon Design **Location:** Long Beach, California, USA **Completion:** 2010 **Photographer:** Feinknopf Photography **Building area:** 11,752 m²

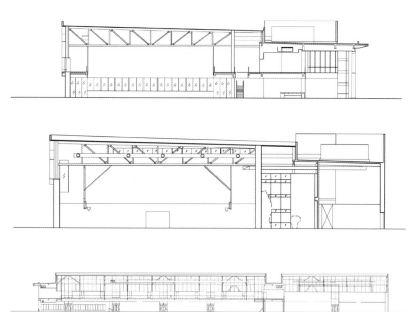

California State University, Long Beach's new 11,752-square-metre Recreation and Wellness Centre, at the campus northeast edge, anchors students' life in a built environment that emphasizes continuity of indoors and outdoors and the belief that health and fitness are essential to academic success. A landscaped entry plaza with an adjoining snack and juice bar is conveniently linked to the campus north-south circulation axis, providing a much-needed student gathering space that is particularly appreciated by evening students making their ways to and from an adjacent parking structure. A walled courtyard includes sand volleyball courts and a recreation pool strategically located to optimise sun exposure as well as operational efficiency.

Activities are organised along an interior street that maximises views between major functions, creating a sense of community and continuous vitality. High-activity spaces such as the 1,858-square-metre cardio/fitness centre enjoy ample views of playing fields and the entry plaza through broad expanses of windows that also serve to transform the building into an illuminative beacon at night. On level 2, a running track surrounds the three-court gym and a portion of the cardio/fitness centre. The large building masses of the building's three-court gymnasium and the two-court MAC abut and mask the adjacent parking garage. Three multipurpose rooms on the second floor, above the locker rooms, are protected from noise and reverberation and enjoy prime views of the pool deck and sand volleyball courts. The building also includes two racquetball courts, a wellness centre, and staff offices.

Design concepts reinforce the university's rich tradition of campus architecture and landscape while remaining true to the ideology of connecting indoor spaces with the outdoors and making indoor exercise replicate the natural, outdoor experience as closely as possible. Employing the campus vocabulary of brick and expressed frame, the building is planned as the first of a new generation of buildings that are more traditionally monumental yet still draw inspiration from the campus's modernist roots. An array of sustainable materials, systems, and strategies make the building eligible for LEED Silver status, including an east-west orientation that helps suffuse the interior with natural light from the north and south.

1. Sand volleyball court
2. Lawn outside the building
3. Plaza

2

1. Lobby
2. Reception hall

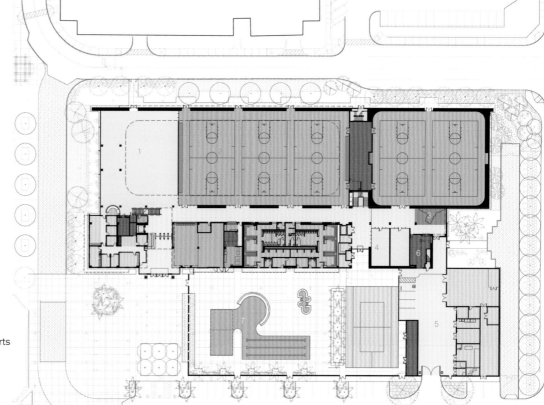

1. Fitness
2. Gymnasium/multi-activities courts
3. Rock climbing wall
4. Racquetball courts
5. Lounge
6. Equipment storage
7. Swimming pool

1. Basketball hall
2. Gym
3. Running track
4. Fitness facilities with running track

East Campus Athletic Village

Designer: David Dymecki, Don Vitters, Jim Gresal, Serge Plishevsky, Steve Shetler **Location:** Troy, NY, USA **Completion:** 2009 **Photographer:** Robert Benson **Site area:** 19,324m²

The new East Campus Athletic Village (ECAV) at Rensselaer is a newly developed area of the campus that provides indoor and outdoor facilities for athletic teams, coaches, staff and Rensselaer community. Phase 1 includes an arena, stadium, outdoor fields and a renovated hockey rink organised along Georgian Terrace, an outdoor pedestrian space that can be used for game-day activities, graduation, and special events. The new complex is divided into strategically placed buildings enclosing the football field, reducing game-day sounds and light glare to neighbourhood areas, while allowing people to filter through the site.

Approaching from the main campus to the south, the arena welcomes students and visitors to the ECAV. The banded masonry gym is wrapped with intersecting metal clad and aluminum curtain wall volumes, which provide views, light, and connection to the stadium. The two-storey lobby houses the student lounge and the Hall of Fame and leads to the gyms, locker rooms, and fitness and sports medicine suites with football field views. The upper level balcony and cafe overlook the Harkness Field and connect to the stadium concourse. The stadium's aluminum screen on its dark textured masonry plinth provides a compelling image. The stadium plinth houses men's and women's home and visiting teams, locker room facilities. It provides first level entry points from Georgian Terrace and second level entry points from the football field. At the third level, the horizontal louvers enclose the open-air concourse leading to concessions, public restrooms, grandstand access, the arena and private access to the upper level VIP and press box. ECAV has achieved LEED Gold Certification.

1. View from the grassland
2. Night view of the concourse

1. View from football ground
2. Concourse

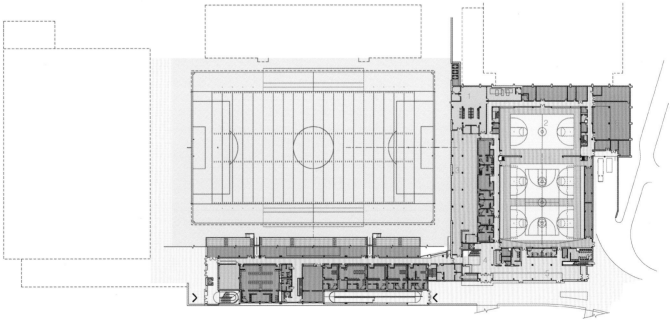

1. Sports medicine
2. Practice gymnasium
3. Strength and conditioning centre
4. Lobby
5. Student Lounge
6. Chiller

1 Passage
2. Interior hall
3. Basketball room

Sports City Hall Bale

Designer: 3LHD **Location:** Bale, Croatia **Completion:** 2006 **Photographer:** 3LHD **Site area:** 3,660 m²

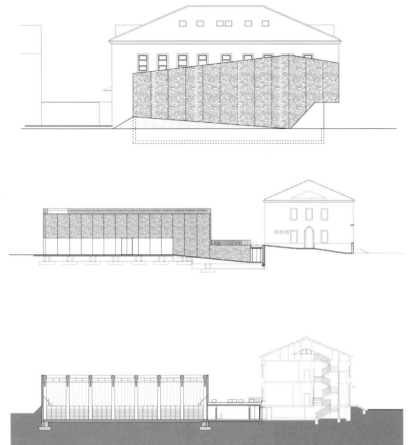

Bale is a small village in Istria peninsula, Croatia with mostly agricultural population of 1,000 people. The project for the new sports hall has been faced with the rich historical, cultural and social Mediterranean context. Therefore any new architectural interpolation had to have a respectful approach to the environment. The solution has been found in interpreting the traditional ways of building by new technologies.

Inspiration for structure has been found in the small traditional stone hut - kažun, a small multifunctional building used as a shelter for shepherds that provide a cool environment in hot weather and insulating against the cold in the winter. Traditionally built without any cement or mortar with carefully selected interlocking stones found on the site this structure is a primitive example of prefabrication present in the Mediterranean since the prehistoric times. The traditional local dry stone wall motif has been used as a template/pattern for the whole surfacing of the sports hall.

On the other hand, being the second largest building after the church, the social importance of the sports hall for the town community is considerable because, besides as a sports venue, it is used as a public facility for various social gatherings, from community meetings, trade fairs to watching World Cup. Actually, the size of the building has been defined by the basketball playground and modified by additional facilities on the gallery: a fitness centre and a sauna, while the low and small locker rooms are planned as a connection element to the school. This connection to the old school with the utility rooms is hidden underground. On the other hand, the private and intimate character of the building is juxtaposed to the open public primary function of the building and its openness by glass fronts to the street.

The sports hall concept has been made to meet the design and construction time schedule of 11 months, which was possible only by using RC prefabricated elements. All the bearing and façade elements of the sports hall have been made from prefabricated elements.

1. Solid exterior wall
2. A roof garden at the back
3. Glass structure below the solid wall

3

1. Overview of the building at night
2. Entrance
3. Handball court

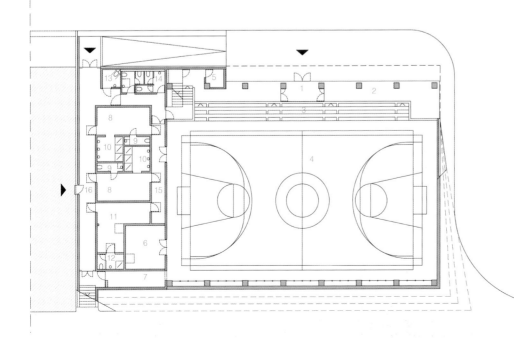

1. Entrance
2. Hall
3. Stands
4. Pitch
5. Mechanical room
6. Equipment store
7. Evacuation corridor
8. Dressing room
9. Sanitary facilities
10. Showers
11. Cabinet + ambulance
12. Sanitary facilities/ teachers
13. Sanitary facilities/disabled persons
14. Sanitary facilities/guests
15. Clean corridor
16. Entrance corridor

University of Arizona Student Recreation Expansion

Designer: Sasaki Associates, Inc. **Location:** Tucson, Arizona, USA **Completion:** 2010 **Photographer:** Timmerman Photography, Inc. **Building area:** 5,017 m²

The new Student Recreation Centre Expansion (SRCE) serves as a destination within the complex; all students and visitors must register in the existing building. The facility is positioned as the "light at the end of the tunnel", relieving a long, internally-focused circulation corridor. The outwardly-focused expansion promotes a purposefully exhibitionist attitude toward recreational programme elements.

As a major hub for student life, the SRCE leverages its most active programme element, the fitness centre, in the most visible and transparent manners possible – activating the 6th Street corridor with a vibrant student presence and allowing interior occupants to view activity outdoors, and vice versa, promoting recreational diversity. The expansion includes the Fitness Centre, Outdoor Adventures and the Multi-use Activity Court (MAC) Gymnasium. A series of outdoor courtyards house rock-climbing "boulders", sand volleyball courts, and outdoor fitness areas.

The courtyard is further defined by two intersecting roof elements providing carefully tuned passive shading. These signature eaves are rendered terra cotta in reference to the core campus' red brick context while materials including weathered steel and concrete masonry reflect the colours and textures of the surrounding Sonoran Desert.

The ecological imperatives of the desert location are addressed throughout the building. The project integrates passive solar orientation, programmed outdoor space, day-lighting strategies, and indoor environmental quality as fundamental properties of the facility. The building both evokes and manifests its sustainable design goals, achieving LEED NC 2.2 Platinum level certification, the first collegiate level recreation facility in the nation to do so. Exceeding the University's expectations, the centre has resulted in a 91% increase in participation (as measured by unique visits) and a 10% increase in membership.

Awarded:

Structural Engineers Association of Arizona, Excellence in Engineering Award, 2010
PCBC Gold Nugget Awards Programme, Award of Merit, Best Public/Private Special Use, 2010

1. Outdoor adventure
2. Courtyard
3. Fitness
4. Sand volleyball
5. Gymnasium

1. View into the inside from windows
2. Rock climbing outdoor

3

1. Light shining from inside
2. Sand volleyball field
3. Gym

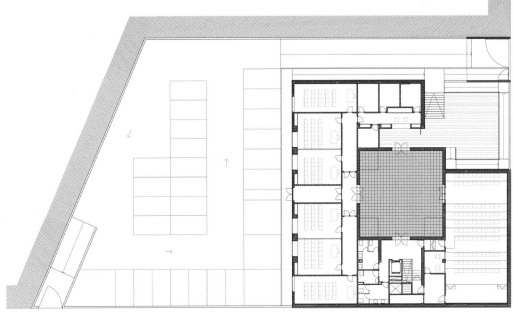

3

1. People could see outdoor view at the facilities next to the window
2. Basketball court
3. Façade details

Drexel University Recreation Centre

Designer: Sasaki Associates, Inc. **Location:** Philadelphia, PA, USA **Completion:** 2010 **Photographer:** Robert Benson Photography, Halkin Photography LLC **Area:** 7, 980 m²

The Drexel campus straddles both sides of Market Street in Philadelphia's University City section. Sasaki's addition to the 1960s-era athletic complex, the Daskalakis Athletic Centre (DAC), accomplishes several institutional and programmatic goals: it increases the university's visual presence along Market Street, integrates existing and new buildings into a unified complex, and groups all of the recreation facilities into a new building wing. Respecting that the DAC is surrounded by one of Drexel's few outdoor landscape spaces, the design also maximises preservation of the site's open space.

The new building wraps around two sides of the DAC building, providing a new urban presence along Market Street. The main façade is treated as a large glazed screen with meandering folds shaded by the extension of the building's floors. The folded enclosure provides alcoves along the exercise areas, where active users and equipments add a sense of colour and movement to the streetscape. The glazed skin is also the result of extensive energy studies. The design is expected to reduce cooling loads by 50% on the south façade and 30% on the east.

At street level the building "interacts" with the passing urban scene: paving patterns echo the angular folds of the building; a café is placed among trees preserved and integrated into the design; and a restaurant engages the larger community as well as students. A previously nondescript corner is brought to life through the combination of a landscaped plaza and the centre's climbing wall framed in glass — a further outward expression of a building housing dynamic activities. All in all, the Daskalakis Athletic Centre provides a perfect recreating area for students of Drexel University, and at the same time makes their campus life more and more diversified.

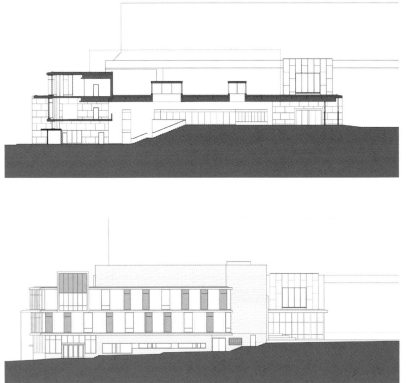

1. Façade along the street
2. Front view
3. Playground in front of the main entrance

3

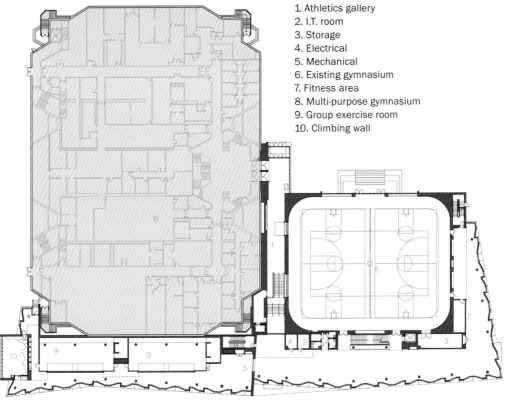

1. Athletics gallery
2. I.T. room
3. Storage
4. Electrical
5. Mechanical
6. Existing gymnasium
7. Fitness area
8. Multi-purpose gymnasium
9. Group exercise room
10. Climbing wall

1. View into the indoor climbing
2. Reception hall
3. Interior basketball room

1 Gymnasium
2. Training room

2

Tianjin Sports Arena

Designer: KSP Jürgen Engel Architekten **Location:** Tianjin, China **Completion:** 2010 **Photographer:** Shuhe Photography, Beijing / KSP Jürgen Engel Architekten **Site area:** 19,620 m²

October 20, 2010 saw the official opening of the Tianjin Sports Arena, which forms part of the campus of the renowned Tianjin University. It serves as a venue for university and national sports events and has room for approx. 5,000 spectators. It was built on behalf of Tianjin University Department of Campus Construction and Planning inline with a design proposal put forward by KSP Jürgen Engel Architekten, Beijing, China.

The building is 120 metres long, 5 metres wide, and located in the northeast of the Tianjin University campus. Situated at the junction between the campus and downtown, the new building is an important link in the urban structure. The Sports Arena has a distinctive feature in the form of a translucent sheath made of gold-coloured perforated sheet steel panels, which form a rhombic structure and emphasize the Arena's dynamic, powerful shape. Punching tools were made specially to produce the perforations, which, with their triangular shape, take up the format of the panels. A special effect adds further emphasis to the spatial depth and the lightness of the metallic façade, which is mounted some four metres in front of the actual outer wall: an enlarged likeness of the structure of the translucent perforated sheet steel façade in the form of a black-and-white print was transferred to the outer wall of the hall. The overlapping of these two levels – the perforated sheet steel façade and the likeness of it – produces a Moiré effect, which is heightened further by the observer moving, and when it is dark, when the space between the façade and the outer wall is artificially lit.

Two spacious foyers open out the Sports Arena in the campus and a busy junction in the direction of downtown Tianjin. The two entrance halls each penetrate the corner of the outer skin and provide access to the building via the narrow sides. The large expanses of glass in the foyer extend almost the entire height of the building (24 metres) and create an entrance that is bright and flooded with light. On the longitudinal sides the glass façades mimic the inclination of the spectator stands. This way the geometry of the hall's interior and the rising spectator stands is also discernible in the design of the façade.

The walls of the entrance halls are bright orange and form an exciting contrast to the open exposed concrete stairs. These lead from the foyer directly up to the spectator stands on the inside of the arena, which have room for some 4,000 spectators. In addition there are 1,000 temporary places on the longitudinal sides of the court. The rows of spectator seats, which, being orange and grey, correspond with the colour of the foyer, flank a 24 x 44-metre basketball or handball court that conforms to the sports' rules. For everyday university purposes the playing area can be divided into two smaller basketball courts or a maximum of 12 badminton courts. All the ancillary rooms such as the changing rooms are located in the levels beneath the stand.

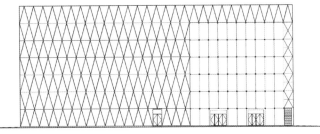

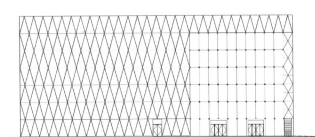

1. Side view of the building
2. Outdoor stairs to the building
3. Façade
4. Back of the building

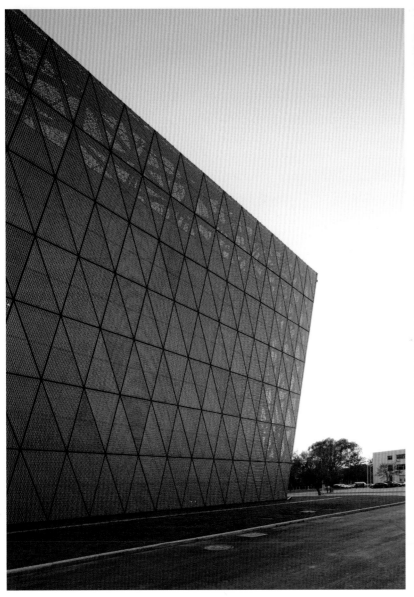

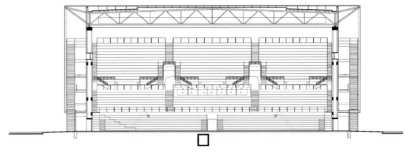

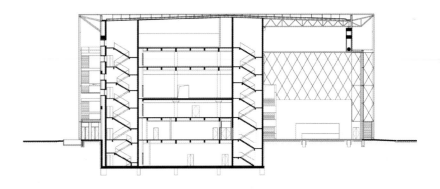

1. Building at night
2. Overview of the building
3. Exterior wall of the building
4. Glass wall shining

1. Sports hall
2. Stairs
3. Entrance hall

1. Athlete lobby
2. Athlete lounge
3. Athlete checking
4. Athlete corridor
5. Visitors entrance hall
6. Temporary seats
7. Arena
8. Jury Lounge
9. Sports equipment storage
10. Computer centre

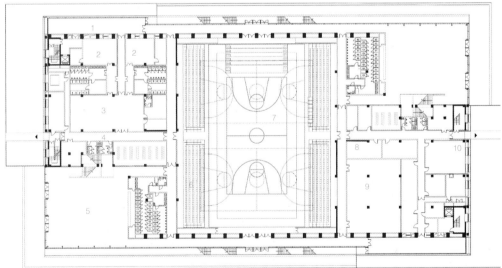

Sollentuna Swimming and Sports Centre Extension

Designer: Rosenberg & Stål Arkitektkontor **Location:** Sollentuna, Sweden **Completion:** 2009
Photographer: Tord-Rikard Söderström **Building area:** Extension 1,340 m²

Sollentuna Swimming and Sports Centre was planned for a renewal and extension with focus on family and play, exercise, rehabilitation and recreation. The first stage consisted of a complete renovation of the existing building and an addition of a new gym.

The renovation had the goal to restore and strengthen qualities from the original building that was rewarded the Kasper Salin Prize in 1975. The central communication of the building was once again opened up and joined to a new entrance to the east. The character of a public building is emphasized and the building has been made more easily oriented.

The original terracotta coloured mosaic of the swimming hall has been replaced with a new mosaic in three green nuances. The pattern origins from an aerial photo of the royal garden of Edsviken, the park can be seen from the swimming pool. One pixel in the image corresponds to a 30 centimetres x30 centimetres unit of mosaic tiles.

The extension building consists of a three-storey gym now forming the highest part of the complex. The three large rooms on each floor opens up to different directions. From the outside the extension stands out as a homogenous steel clad volume connecting to the characteristic roof of the existing building. The large glass partition to the west slants to give room to the flow of visitors walking up to the new main entrance.

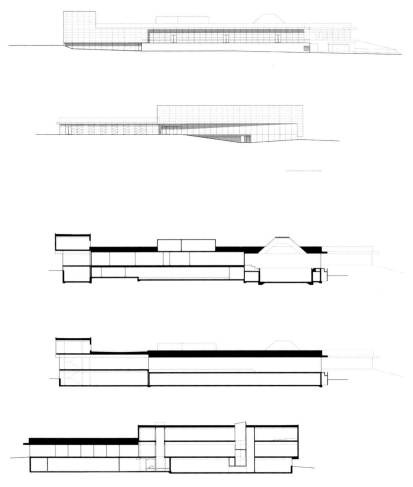

1. Building with surrounding landscape
2. Entrance
3. View into gym

2

3

1. Exterior stairs to the entrance
2. Bowling entrance

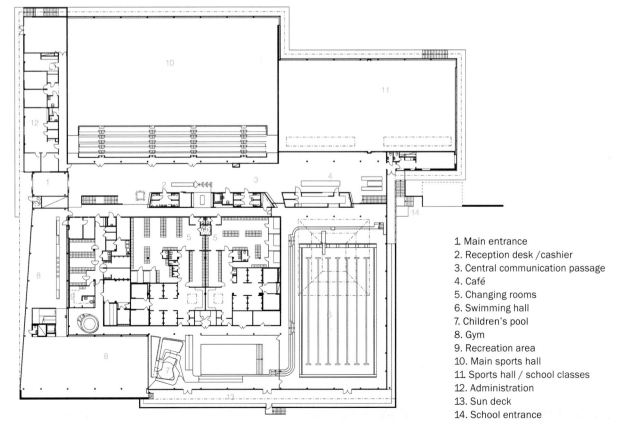

1. Main entrance
2. Reception desk /cashier
3. Central communication passage
4. Café
5. Changing rooms
6. Swimming hall
7. Children's pool
8. Gym
9. Recreation area
10. Main sports hall
11. Sports hall / school classes
12. Administration
13. Sun deck
14. School entrance

1. Gym
2. Transparent features
3. Swimming pool

Chimo Aquatic and Fitness Centre

Designer: Hughes Condon Marler Architects **Location:** Coquitlam, Canada **Completion:** 2006
Photographer: Martin Tessler **Site area:** 3,214 m² **Building area:** 3,550 m²

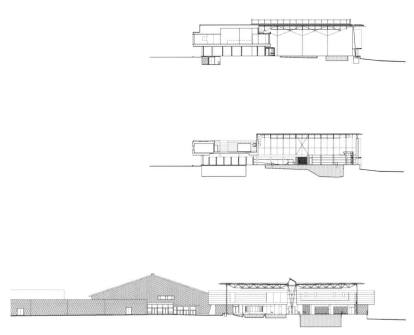

The new Chimo Aquatic & Fitness Centre is the first phase of the renewal of the Coquitlam Recreation and Sports Centre. It is located at the centre of a campus of public facilities in South Coquitlam in Greater Vancouver on the high point of land in an area that is predominantly single-family housing. The City recognised the importance of the project by supporting the concept that the building would be the centrepiece of the campus, expressing a commitment to health, well-being, sustainability and accessibility.

The massing concept envisions the building in two distinct parts, a natatorium and support spaces. The natatorium, which comprises almost half of the 3,550 square metres programme, includes a six lane 25-metre lap pool, leisure pool, warm-up lap pool, hot pool, steam and sauna. The support spaces accommodate the remainder of the programme, including change rooms, mechanical rooms and fitness areas, and are located in a three-storey linear bar structure along one side of the natatorium.

The natatorium is the "front room" of the centre and is situated directly adjacent Poirier Street, with a reduced setback giving this space the strongest street presence of all facilities in the area. The support functions housed in the three-storey bar structure are located on the opposite wall of the natatorium away from the street, but adjacent the future concourse that will serve all of the facilities in the recreation and sports centre. This massing strategy allows the aquatic centre to be a free-standing project while accommodating future phases of the recreation centre development.

The large north and south glazed walls of the two-storey glass natatorium cube are highly visible when approaching. The reading of the glass volume is reinforced by the floating screen wall along Poirier Street. The roof is split into two planes, divided by a central skylight and an array of solar panels further expressing the natatorium as a glass cube nested in a series of planer elements supported and anchored by the solid volumes of the support functions. The project succeeds in incorporating sustainable design to a level that demonstrates Coquitlam's leadership and commitment to sustainability.

Awarded:
Lieutenant Governor of British Columbia Awards for Architecture 2009
Athletic Business Facility of Merit Award 2009

1. The building in the surrounding landscape
2. Back façade
3. View from the street

1. Façade
2. Parking lot
3. Surrounding landscape
4. Entrance

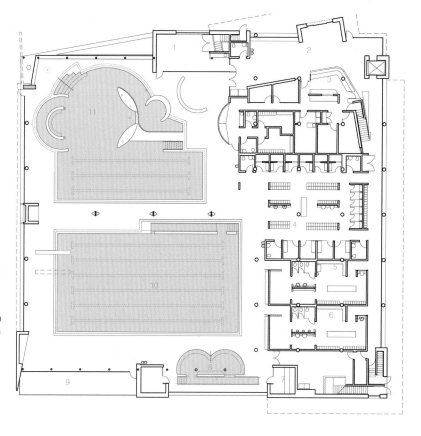

1. Multi-purpose room
2. Lobby
3. Admin + staff areas
4. Universal change room
5. Women's change room
6. Men's change room
7. Sauna
8. Hot pool
9. Sundeck
10. 25m lap pool
11. Leisure pool

1. Children's pool
2. The unique roof structure above the pool
3. Sunshine spread into interior of the swimming hall
4. Swimming track

1. Stairs up to the gym
2. Reception
3. Weight training

Birkerød Sports and Leisure Centre

Designer: schmidt hammer lassen architects **Location:** Birkerød, Denmark **Completion:** 2008
Photographer: Adam Mørk **Building area:** 8,000 m² new build & 1,200 m² refurbishment

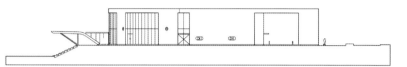

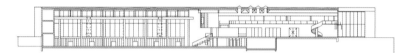

Birkerød Sports Centre in Rudersdal Municipality close to Copenhagen is a modern sports and culture complex that sets new standards in terms of both practicality and architecture.

Fitness, yoga, team handball, concerts and other cultural events – all in a setting of one modern sculptural entity designed by schmidt hammer lassen architects. The façade's long sweeping lines and striking sculptural roof contours evoke a sense of movement and activity – creating a direct link between the building's design and its core function. Upon entering, the space appears bright, airy and open. The interiors are filled with natural light, and transparency creates a sense of permeability and activity.

The sports and activity centre is a multifunctional structure. The new building includes a large multipurpose hall with enough space to accommodate two handball courts with accompanying mobile spectator stands, as well as a V.I.P. lounge. The centre also houses two smaller halls. This means the complex can accommodate major sporting events, concerts and other cultural events, but also be adapted for school sporting events and local sports initiatives requiring smaller, more intimate settings.

The new centre is located in the midst of existing football pitches and the old public swimming baths, both of which have received a facelift, and now include a new grandstand for the football pitch and a full-scale remodelling of the public swimming baths, which are now significantly larger. This bridges the gap between the existing sports and recreational facilities to create a more coherent offer for sports and cultural activities in Birkerød. The new centre represents a quantum leap from the typical Danish sports facilities typically characterised by large rectangular halls with laminated wood arches. Birkerød Sports Centre is very different in terms of both flexibility and design. The aesthetics and design of Birkerød Sports Centre are immediately distinctive – with its long curves it is a bold and beautiful sculptured focal point for the local community, combining sports, cultural and recreational activities in the Birkerød area. The series of façades are decorated by graphic artist Astrid Krog, Denmark. The black circles form interconnected patterns when the louvres are closed and daylight shines in through the oblong window sections.

Awarded:
2006 Façade System Selected for Inclusion in the Danish Ministry of Culture's Canon for Design and Handicrafts
2008 World Architecture Festival, shortlisted

1. Façade at night
2. Glass façade shining in the daylight

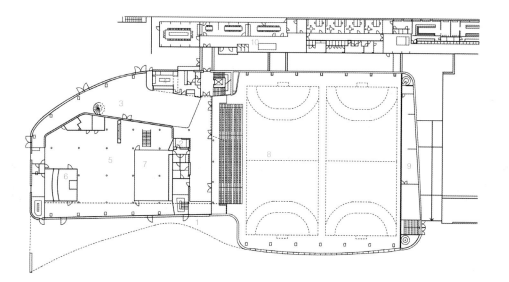

1. Main entrance
2. Reception
3. Foyer
4. Café
5. Fitness
6. Spinning
7. Aerobic
8. Multipurpose hall
9. Depot
10. Stadium-existing

2

1. View into the interior gym
2. Light circles on the exterior roof

1. The auditorium
2. Playing court
3. Lobby
4. Swimming hall

Curtin Stadium

Designer: CHRISTOU Design Group **Location:** Perth, Australia **Completion:** 2009 **Photographer:** CHRISTOU Design Group **Building area:** 5,653m²

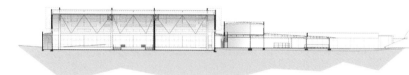

Completed in 2009, Curtin Stadium is testament to CHRISTOU's ability to deliver a state-of-the-art sporting and events facility.

The Curtin Stadium is an iconic structure well placed at the front of the University's "dress circle" buildings. It is airy, full of light and ideally suited to the many varied events it will host. Its innovative architectural design and attractive interiors provide a setting that creates a lasting impression on visitors, highlighting Curtin University's commitment to sustainable design and technological excellence.

To ensure long term value for money, the sleek white metallic structure was cladded in maintenance-free Alucobond. Environmental initiatives in particular, cross ventilation and natural illumination have also sought to reduce utility costs.

With a total enclosed area of 5,653 square metres, Curtin Stadium houses a gym, spin room, aerobics studio, private women's gym, offices, administration, reception and café, while its main feature is a vast 2,100-square-metre flexible events, expo and recreation hall space that does the work of three buildings. For formal occasions, it is a graduation hall holding an audience of 2,500, with guest seating for 1,760, comprising two banks of fully retractable tiered rows. A speedy conversion adapts the area to an examination hall seating for 1,000 students, or again to a fully-equipped sports centre providing multiple courts for basketball, netball, volleyball and badminton.

The project incorporated a number of ESD techniques including passive solar design, natural light and ventilation, building management, material selection and façade shading to achieve environmental objectives of the client.

CHRISTOU developed a clever and responsive linear plan, which detailed a north-south orientation to provide for maximum sun control and natural ventilation. To maximise the benefits of this orientation, the design also included sun louvres or mesh to shade glass façades, and colonnades and verandas to provide external shade. These façades provide maximum natural ventilation and natural light into the complex.

Awarded:
AIA (WA Chapter) Design Award for Interior Architecture, 2010
Best Commercial Project Award, 2010
Entry into AIA National Awards

1. Overview of the building at night
2. Entrance
3. Neat façade of the building

1

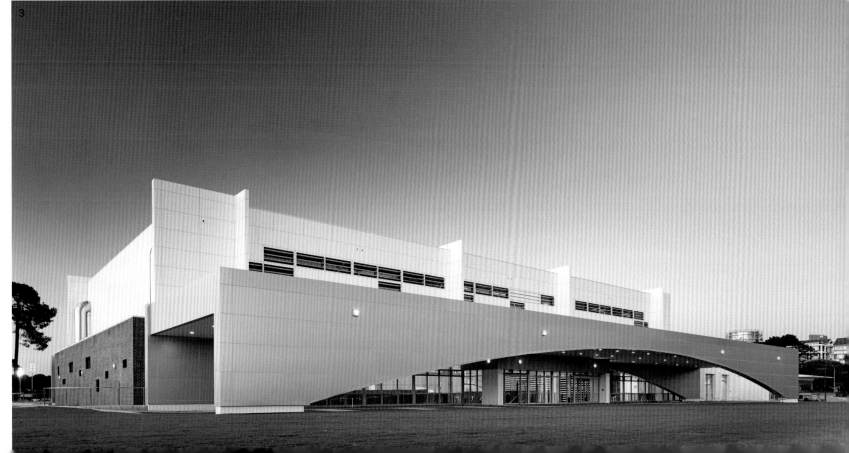

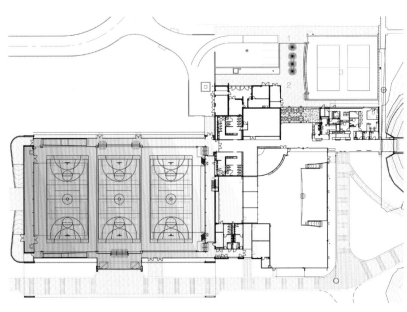

1. Main entrance
2. Lobby
3. Fitness centre
4. Cafe
5. Basketball hall

2

1. Lobby sculpture
2. Fitness centre
3. Relaxation area

3

1. Basketball hall
2. Basketball hall details
3. Auditorium

Deodoro Sports Complex

Designer: BCMF Architects **Location:** Rio de Janeiro, Brazil **Completion:** 2007 **Photographer:** BCMF Arquitetos/Jomar Bragança, Bruno Carvalho, Kaká Ramalho **Site area:** 1,000,000 m² **Building area:** 100,000 m²

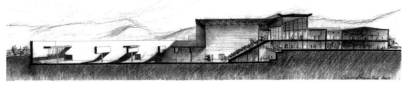

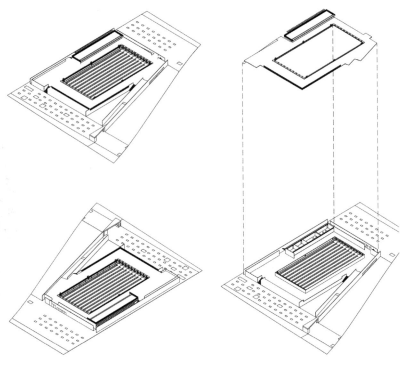

The Deodoro region has the highest demographic of youth within the greater metropolitan region of Rio de Janeiro, and it is one of the poorest zones of the city. Until recently this area lacked the infrastructure and facilities to support the needs of the population. The development of facilities for the 2007 Pan American Games has encouraged the less privileged youth of this region to actively participate in sport. The addition of specifically targeted facilities, most notably the new attraction for the 2016 Olympics, the X-Park Precinct, will provide strong social and sport development legacy and opportunities.

The Deodoro Sports Complex was designed for the Pan-American Games with an awareness that a similar competition venue and programme would be applied to a future Olympic Games (Rio 2016), including the shooting, equestrian, archery, hockey and modern pentathlon facilities, and also permanent training areas for all major national, regional and international shooting competitions, in the same cluster. Therefore, the National Sports Shooting Centre (NSC), the National Equestrian Centre (NEC) and the swimming pool of the National Centre of Modern Pentathlon (MNP) already meet international standards, and will need minor adjustments and complements.

The cluster is already an important legacy, which has successfully triggered the renewal and further development of this important vector of the city. The project deals with the complex issues of a unique suburban context comprising a military district, a densely populated favela, a dilapidated industrial area, as well as a large expanse of native vegetation. With its new attractions and improvements, the new Deodoro Sports Complex will be definitely a formidable world-class legacy of high-performance sports for this region, forming a cluster with great potential for catalyzing a general revitalisation of a significant suburban area of the city.

Awarded:

Golden Medal at the First IAKS LAC Award (International Association for Sports and Leisure Facilities / Section Latin America and Caribbean).

1. Aerial view
2. National Equestrian Centre – stables
3. Centre of Modern Pentathlon

1

1. The grandstand building
2. Outdoor shooting area covered by a timber frame
3. Eastern entrance view at night

1. National Sports Shooting Centre
2. National Archery Centre
3. National Centre of Modern Pentathlon
4. National Equestrian Centre

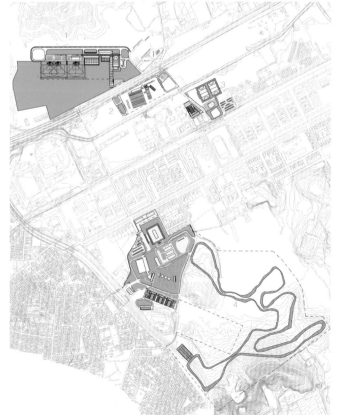

1. The indoor shooting hall
2. Central corridor

2

Ronald McDonald Centre

Designer: Fact Architects **Location:** Amsterdam, the Netherlands **Completion:** 2010 **Photographer:** Luuk Kramer **Site area:** 5.2 hectares

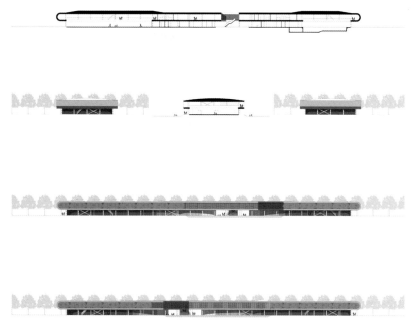

The Ronald McDonald Centre is a sports centre for disabled children. It is located in a typical Dutch countryside on the edge of Amsterdam. The municipality of Amsterdam donated the beautiful, and well connected location and a new parking lot. The design of the Centre matches perfectly with the natural and green surroundings.

An important design goal was to communicate a sense of security to children and adolescents, and at the same time the feeling of being a top athlete. By the way, the Centre is designed that everybody is both spectator and audience. The centre of the complex is the main building, wedged between two oval arenas, which are sunk in the elevated terrain and are surrounded by trees and grandstand stairs.

The first floor offers views of all outdoor and indoor activities. In this part of the building's several recreational functions are situated. Here you can meet, eat and drink, watch movies and playing computer games and at the same time watch other children playing sports. For orientation, colours are being used. The floors per part of the building are of different colours. The indoor hall, the fitness room and the dojo are green, the swimming pool is blue and the grandstands with the restaurants and offices are red.

Due to the enthusiasm of the sponsors, a high level of innovations and special applications of materials and technologies have been achieved. A great example of new technology is the floor of the indoor sports hall. It is the very first floor in the world with so-called LED-lines. The lines can be switch on to the sport, needed on that moment. The other lines are then invisible. There are special ceilings, of "ball proof" metal mesh, and glass sliding doors developed. Lockers are operated by a finger scan and the pools have movable floors.

Safety is very important in this sports centre. The corridors are situated at the glass façade for close contact and a good overview. The swimming pool has a drowning detection system. With infrared cameras there is a 24-hour watch at the pool.

The Centre is durable in many ways. The main building is constructed in a way that it creates a liberal floor plan, giving the opportunity to the change areas more easily in the future. During the construction, all waste has been re-used. Spare warmth of the swimming pool is being re-used. The cantilever construction of the first floor gives a natural shade in the sports hall and pool hall.

1. Building façade
2. Entrance of the main building
3. View into the interior swimming pool

2

3

1. Leisure hall
2. Green corridor
3. Red corridor above the swimming pool

3

1. Sports hall
2. Swimming pool
3. Dressing room / toilets
4. Fitness
5. Dojo
6. First aid
7. Lift platform
8. Information desk
9. Dressing rooms
10. Competition pool
11. Multipurpose pool
12. Gallery
13. Technical room
14. Kitchen
15. Computer room
16. Theatre podium
17. Hobby room
18. Clubhouse / restaurant
19. Toilets
20. Offices

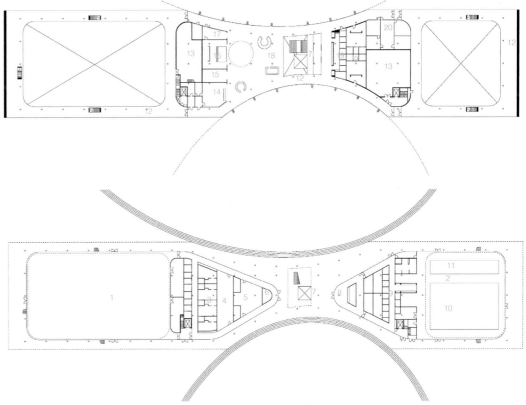

1. Sports hall, with LED lines
2. Swimming pool

Index

3LHD
T: +385 1 2320200
F: +385 1 2320100

AGM
T: + 381 11 3223 287
F: + 381 11 3223 283

Allen Jack + Cottier
T: +61 2 9311 8222
F: +61 2 9311 8200

ALSOP SPARCH-Archial Group plc
T: +44 (0)20 7580 0400
T: +44 (0)20 7580 6680

Atelier Mauch gmbh
Email: office@ateliermauch.at

AXS SATOW inc.
T: 010-62792194

barbosa & guimarães-josé antónio barbosa · pedro lopes guimarães
T: 00 351 229 363 022
F: 00 351 229 363 024

BATLLE I ROIG ARQUITECTES
T: 93 457 98 84
F: 93 459 12 24

BCMF Architects
T: +55 31 3281 2707
F: +5531 3194 3051

BIAD
T: 010-88043999
F: 010-68034041

Cannon Design
T: 716.774.3494
F: 716.773.5909

CHRISTOU Design Group
T: +61 8 9285 6888
F: + 618 9285 6893

Claudio Lucchin & architetti associate
T: +39 0471 502465
F: +39 0471 502481

Enota
T: +386 1 438 67 40
F: +386 1 438 67 45

Fact Architects
T: +31(0)204633793

Francisco José Mangado Beloqui
T: 948 27 62 02
F: 948 17 65 05

Franz zt gmbh
T: 0676-897 107 100

Geninasca Delefortrie SA
T: 032 729 99 60
F: 032 729 99 69

Giancarlo Mazzanti & Felipe Mesa
T: (57) 1 3406564-2326309

gmp-von Gerkan, Marg and Partners Architects
T: +49.40.88 151 0
F: +49.40.88 151 177

Hughes Condon Marler Architects
T: 604 732 6620
F: 604 732 6695

IDOM-ACXT
T: +34 91 444 11 63
F: +34 91 447 31 87

JAAM architects
T: +34 944 02 96 54

KSP Jürgen Engel Architekten
T: +49(0)69.94 43 94-0
F: +49(0)69.94 43 94-38

Nadel Architects
T: 310 826 2100
F: 310 826 0182

Populous
T: +64 9 379 3063
F: +64 9 379 9129

Reiach and Hall Architects
T: 0131 225 8444
F: 0131 225 5079

Rosenbergs Architects
T: 08-54587100
F: 08-54587120

Saïa Barbarese Topouzanov Architectes
T: 514 866 2085
F: 514 874 0233

Salto AB
T: +372 682 5222

Sasaki Associates, Inc.
T: 617 926 3300
F: 617 924 2748

schmidt hammer lassen architects
T: +45 87 32 53 16
M: +45 20 20 37 14

Shuhei Endo Architect Institute
T: 81-6-6354-7456
F: 81-6-6354-7457

SIA Substance
T: +371 29265568

Tabanlioglu Architects
T: +90 212 2512111
F: +90 212 2512332

UPI-2M
T: +385 (0) 1 3772 089
F: +385 (0) 1 3701 435

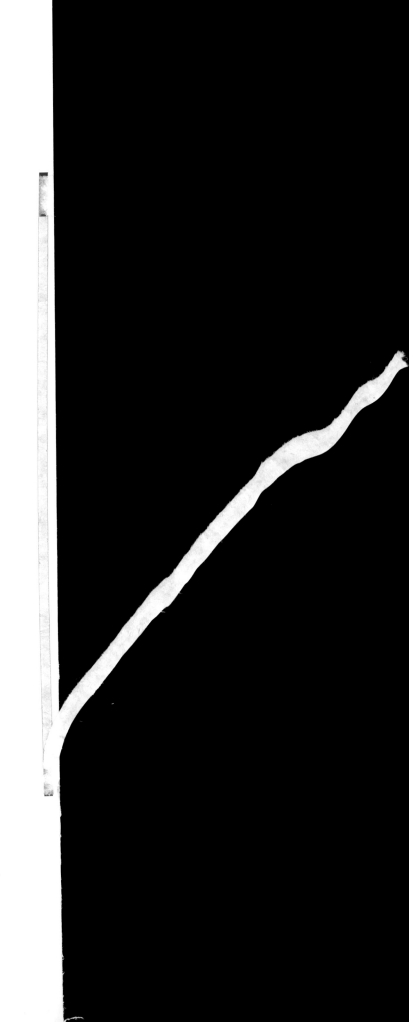

©2010 by Design Media Publishing Limited
This edition published in June 2012

Design Media Publishing Limited
20/F Manulife Tower
169 Electric Rd, North Point
Hong Kong
Tel: 00852-28672587
Fax: 00852-25050411
E-mail: Kevinchoy@designmediahk.com
www.designmediahk.com

Editing: LI Chunmei
Proofreading: YIN Qian
Design/Layout: ZHAO Cong

ISBN 978-988-15450-1-5

Printed in China